Presence After Trauma

D1452066

Also by Sonia Connolly

Wellspring of Compassion: Self-Care for Sensitive People Healing from Trauma

Presence After Trauma

Reconcile with Yourself and the World

Sonia Connolly

Sundown Healing Arts
Portland, Oregon

Published by Sundown Healing Arts, Portland, Oregon
SundownHealingArts.com
Requests for permission to make copies of any part of the work
can be submitted to permissions@sundownhealingarts.com.
For bulk orders, write to orders@sundownhealingarts.com.
File under: SELF-HELP/Post-Traumatic Stress Disorder (PTSD)
Printed in the United States of America

Cover photo, Crystal Springs Rhododendron Garden,
Portland, Oregon: Sonia Connolly
Chapter heading illustrations: Laurel Purdy
Illustration credits continued on page 277

Library of Congress Control Number: 2016915723
ISBN-13: 978-0-9839038-1-9
FIRST EDITION
This publication is not intended as a substitute for the advice of
health care professionals. Internet addresses were accessible at
the time this book went to press. Content of referenced websites
is solely that of their sponsors and does not necessarily reflect
the opinions of the author of this book.

Client stories are fictionalized composites of common patterns
seen in sessions.

For all the folks working to make the world a better place in small and large ways, especially those who are interrupting legacies of generational trauma.

Acknowledgments

Thanks to Robyn Posin for ongoing encouragement at each step of this book's creation, including detailed feedback.

Thanks to David Mitchell for proofreading and many conversations.

Thanks to Carrie Mook Bridgman for copy editing and long friendship.

Thanks to each client who courageously shared your process with me in session.

Thanks to each person who responded to my newsletter or first book to tell me how an article touched you.

Contents

Introduction: Welcome Back

Years into your healing work, you might feel that you have largely come back to yourself, and at the same time wonder why you still have trauma-related problems. Or, you might be just starting out, wanting a peek into what lies ahead.

Some things have gotten better, but perhaps not the one goal you set your heart on achieving at the beginning of your process, close relationships or freedom from chronic pain or a steady income or being "normal." Along the way, you have worked very hard and wondered what is wrong with you that your life is not yet perfectly managed. No one seems to talk about the fact that untraumatized people do not manage their lives perfectly either, nor the fact that injuries from trauma can be healed, but not erased.

This book is a non-judgmental companion for your healing process after the initial crisis is over.*

You have found some support that works for you, although support might be an ongoing struggle. You are familiar with your survival tools like denial, dissociation, and

---

* For more on the beginning of the healing process, see my previous book *Wellspring of Compassion: Self-Care for Sensitive People Healing from Trauma*, or <u>TraumaHealed.com/articles/by-topic/</u>.

that loud Inner Critic, and have acquired some alternatives that work better in the present. The old tools do still pop up, though. You have practices for connecting with yourself and providing for your needs, longings, and sensitivities as best you can.

You know how your system responds to anxiety, flash-backs, and other Post-Traumatic Stress Disorder (PTSD) symptoms. You can bear witness to painful memories, and have at least a general idea of your past history.

You sense your preferences and boundaries, and can communicate about them clearly. That does not stop some people from violating them. You recognize emotional abuse, victim-blaming, and other subtle forms of abuse, and avoid them when you can.

Some aspects of your living space are just the way you like them, and others are still a challenge. You have created routines and traditions that suit you. You are struggling more with present-time issues than the past, although you can see how the past still affects you.

How can you reconcile with the present you have, rather than the easier, cozier present you deserve? How can you reconcile with who you are in this moment?

My goal for healing from trauma was to become present. I thought there was a magic threshold of presence that would heal my physical symptoms, smooth my relationships with others, and transform my relationship with myself.

Over time I discovered that presence is a gradient, not a threshold. After more than two decades of becoming more present in my body, each new awareness feels like I am just beginning.

While presence is better than its alternative, absence, it does not fix nearly as much as I thought. Instead, it tells me there is nothing wrong with me and I do not need fixing. Presence gives me a fierce defense when people deny my reality. I am right here paying attention! At the same time presence makes room for uncertainty, ambiguity, and internal conflict.

Trauma fractures us from ourselves. Presence is the antidote. Being present does not erase or undo trauma . That is dissociation, numbness. Presence includes trauma's narratives and effects, without being hijacked by them.

Presence can be drenched in pain, and it can also be playful, pleasurable. Pleasure can be hard to allow if it feels unfamiliar, dangerous, or shameful. Consider being present for tiny bits of pleasure at a time.

Becoming present is an ongoing exploration of willingness to accept what is, and willingness to allow it to change. Over time, we find ways to reconcile with ourselves as we are right now.

To reconcile with the world, we have to reconcile with unfairness and systemic injustice. We received unfair harm in the form of trauma and abuse. We did not get the help and care we needed then, and we may not be getting everything we need now. We also received unfair advantages in the form of resources that helped us survive and heal.

We find our individual reasons to keep trying, keep living, keep holding on until the next shift that might make things better. We find parts of our world that bring us joy, and make choices to move toward more of what we want. As we regain our balance in the present, we can turn some of our energy toward supporting others with their struggles.

You can read this book as a continuous whole, or dip in and out, focusing on the topics that are most alive for you right now. If you feel anxious, impatient, or bored, you can take a break or skip the parts that are difficult for you.

As you read, listen to your body and notice what is true for you with gentle awareness. Tune in to your experience when you have an uninterrupted block of time to yourself, or in bits and pieces as you go about your day, whenever you have time to think and feel.

Overview. These themes weave through all the articles, and group them into sections.

1. **Healing Tools.** We want to heal faster, and at the same time, healing needs to be gently respectful of our boundaries, needs, and vulnerabilities.

2. **Acceptance.** As a daily companion, the balm of acceptance allows every aspect of our experience to be as it is, including demands for things to be different.

3. **Body.** You do not have to improve before deserving to be present in your body, just as your body does not have to improve to deserve your presence. You already belong together.

4. **Trauma Effects.** When we understand the physical and emotional effects of our trauma histories, we can manage them more skillfully.

5. **Self-Trust.** Over time, we rebuild trust in our perceptions, our viewpoint, our wisdom, and our effectiveness in the world.

6. **Hard Times.** We continue to encounter individual abusive interactions, systemic injustice, and personal defeats no matter how healed we get.

7. **Relating.** When we come out of emergency mode, we can once again perceive and send the subtle signals of relating.

Check the **Glossary** for definitions of unfamiliar terms.

1: Healing Tools

Presence cannot be forced. It can be invited, awaited, practiced. Being tricked into presence does harm, disrespecting the body's wise limits on contact with unhealed past trauma.

Trauma is fast and overwhelming. Healing needs to be gently respectful of our boundaries, needs, and vulnerabilities. Healing is gradual and uneven, full of long plateaus, incremental changes, and sudden shifts.

We want change, because we want to heal faster. We fear change, because it brings new challenges and losses. Much of healing is about finding ways to be with our experience right now, connecting with present resources and witnessing past distress.

We can investigate and balance energy systems of the body from different perspectives, viewing them as chakras or Kabbalah's sefirot.

The Power of Gentle

We instinctively approach a frightened animal with slow, gentle movements and a soft voice. We show that we mean no harm, and give the animal time to decide if and how to approach us.

Traumatized humans need the same gentle approach.

Illusion of urgency. Trauma leaves behind an agitated nervous system and a body on high alert. Everything feels intensely urgent, including healing from PTSD. It has to happen now, by any means necessary!

Practitioners often share this urgency, applying strong treatments and pushing through clients' resistance. The client's nervous system, already braced for danger, naturally interprets this approach as an invasive threat.

Pathway to calmness. Gentleness gives an agitated nervous system a pathway to calmness, offering a spacious reminder that safety still exists. A traumatic event is too fast, overwhelming, out of control. Trauma treatment needs to be slow enough to return control to the client. Treatment that overwhelms the client "for their own good" is re-traumatizing.

Moving slowly can be the only way to get there. Pushing more quickly creates a demand to appear healed, using up reserves of energy instead of replenishing them. The sense of emergency continues, along with surrender to external demands.

Patience for the process. Intensity of treatment might be driven by a desire for visible progress. Gentleness requires patience and trust in the process. Similarly, when one sits quietly near a frightened animal, not much is happening on the surface, but nervous systems are communicating and observing each other attentively.

Survivors are already off-balance, coping with a transformed, threatening world. Honor survival skills rather than treating them as pathology. From inside, the trauma-reaction closet appears life-saving. Prying open the door and forcibly extracting someone is neither respectful nor healing. With patience, the door will open.

Contained with awareness. Gentle practitioners work to remain grounded, calm, and aware. Self-awareness allows emotions and reactions to be set aside, creating a clear container for the client's process. Client-awareness allows just the right amount of emotional and physical pressure to make contact without pushing. Gentle practitioners hold space, providing a steady point of reference that offers an anchor in the present.

Trauma ruptures boundaries when it violates physical and emotional safety. During healing, clear boundaries provide a sense of safety and refuge. Both brain and body need to know what to expect. Practitioners cannot demand trust, only offer trustworthy behavior in a peaceful, reliable environment.

Clients do their best to express their needs while searching for practitioners.

- I need help, not fixing.
- I'm injured, not broken.
- I want to feel better and I need to be accepted as I am right now.

Acceptance allows change*. When we make room for feelings of agitation and lack of safety, the nervous system can connect with the present rather than being stuck in past trauma. When we demand change, we push the feelings farther away, out of contact.

Paradoxically, the only leverage for future change is in present acceptance. We cannot simply order the nervous system to be calmer. If we stop barking orders at it to be different, it might calm of its own accord. One of the best doorways to change is, "You can be that way as long as you need to."

---

* See "2: Acceptance" on page 41 for more about this important healing tool.

Heal Around the Edges

As you may remember from getting scraped knees as a child, physical wounds heal from the outside in, at the borders with healthy tissue, where they receive the resources needed to rebuild.

Trauma heals at the borders, too. Somatic Experiencing®, developed by Peter Levine and expanded by Diane Poole Heller, introduces helpful tools to navigate the border between traumatic memory and present time. When we have access to our present resources, we can put traumatic events in context, gradually reducing their power over us. Alternating between a sense of safety and higher levels of stress associated with trauma allows the body to gently discharge stored tension.

Long-term trauma and neglect. Somatic Experiencing applies most directly to acute trauma like a car crash or rape. It works more slowly and indirectly with long-term trauma, where much of the damage comes from neglect and missing resources over a long period of time. If it feels like a technique does not apply, you can skip it, or see if it sparks a tangent for you that does apply.

For pervasive childhood trauma, comfortable calm might be an unfamiliar state. The nervous system might need to gradually learn how to find calm by building stability in the present, and taking it in a little at a time.

Takara's crash. Takara's bike went flying when the car collided with her, and she landed hard on the pavement.

Witnesses immediately clustered around her and a woman put a comforting hand on her shoulder. They encouraged her to lie still, giving her body a chance to react to the impact. Later, she worked through lingering effects with the following techniques.

The goal is to feel better. We tend to believe that more discomfort means more progress. In trauma healing, the opposite is true. The goal is to feel better, rather than being numb or terrified. We need the same attuned care as a crabby infant, inquiring into what we need to feel better, and doing our best to provide it. Enough food, water, rest, and a peaceful environment can go a long way. Gentle rocking and comforting touch can help, too.

Tool: Anchor in present resources. Begin by taking inventory of present-time resources. Take note of present safety, shelter, support, and strength. What do you enjoy about your life now? What do others receive from you that you might also be able to give to yourself? How do others meet your needs? It is worth digging for answers if they do not immediately float up.

As you work with past trauma, bring in awareness of your resources when you start to feel overwhelmed. Bring in the sense of an ally, whether present, past, or imagined. How would it feel to have someone sitting with you who wants you to feel better?

It has been a month since Takara's crash. She looks around her apartment, and notes that she feels safe within its walls. Her friends have given her rides to medical appointments and helped her cook meals while her broken collarbone heals. Takara has felt jittery since the crash, feeling uneasy when she goes outside and finding it hard to sleep. When she focuses on her present sense of safety, she senses more ease in her body, and breathes more deeply.

Tool: Find a sense of safety. One border around trauma is time. We can look at a time before the trauma began, and a time when it clearly ended. Sometimes, the answer to "When did you first realize you were safe?" is, "I haven't (yet)." We flee our bodies during trauma, and miss that the emergency is over. Noticing the details of the present can help bring the realization that the worst of the trauma is over.

Takara thinks about the sunny morning of her crash. She was on her way downtown, enjoying the cool air and the strength in her legs as she biked to work. Her body relaxes as she remembers, followed by angry tears about the sudden loss of that enjoyment. When they pass, she feels calmer, less jittery.

After the crash, she first realized she was safe when she started to get up and the woman with her urged her to lie still. As she thinks back, she remembers the nearby construction workers who directed traffic around her, and feels their concerned protection. Warmth moves through her and she trembles for a while, releasing stored stress.

Tool: Put the threat far away. Another border around trauma is space. You can mentally put the threat far away, restrained in some way, and notice how your body responds. Notice the difference between any remaining present-time threats, and the traumatic threats of the past. In this moment, your life is not in danger.

For complex ongoing trauma, the threats might be more abstract, like the threat of abandonment. Putting the threat farther away can let you feel the relative safety of the present.

Takara puts the car that hit her on a different street, so they would not cross paths. She feels her hunched shoulders soften, and her head turn more freely. Again she trembles for a while as her body responds to the renewed sense of safety.

Tool: Comfortable to uncomfortable. A core trauma healing technique is to move back and forth across the line from comfortable to uncomfortable, keeping your stress level manageable. If you are flooded with flashbacks, you might need outside help to find resources and calmness.

One way to alternate comfort and discomfort is put a threat far enough away to feel safe, and then gradually allow it nearer. Pause when you notice your stress level increase, and return to your resources.

When Takara imagines that the car is approaching her again, she tenses and breathes shallowly. She looks around her quiet apartment and focuses on a favorite painting on the wall to give herself time to calm again.

After discharging stress this way several times, she can see the car's approach, and feels her muscles organize to brake hard and swerve to avoid it. Giving her body a chance to sense into a successful escape resolves a lot of distress around the crash, even though her collarbone is still broken. Afterwards, she no longer feels the need to avoid the intersection where she was hit.

Tool: Add resources. Another way to dial down the intensity of a traumatic event is to add resources. We know what really happened, but we can change how we carry it by editing the story. Add allies, protection, healing energy, or anything else that feels right.

Takara adds protective armor with a soft inner layer, so that when the car hits her, she bounces on the pavement, unharmed. Now, when she thinks of the crash, her body stays calm. She looks around the scene in her memory, and notices the driver's white, terrified face. She moves from rage at his thoughtless acceleration toward a yellow light, to a more peaceful forgiveness. Her jitters settle down, and she sleeps well that night.

Tool: Edges of memory. Traumatic memory is stored in scattered fragments of sensory impressions rather than in continuous narrative form. When we want to retrieve more information about a traumatic event, we can put gentle attention to the edges of what we know. As we use our tools to release stress, we make room to reassemble the shards of memory. New details and perspectives may continue to surface over time.

As Takara's body calmed from the initial terror, rage, and pain, she retrieved memories of protection and care from others. They had been there all along, but were not accessible until her stress level decreased.

Less is more. Trauma is overwhelming. Trauma healing needs to be gentle and manageable. Touching into the edges of a traumatic event and then returning to safe ground allows the safe ground to expand, eventually healing the whole wound and resolving traumatic symptoms.

Choose an Easier Road

I rode my bike down a freeway on-ramp the other day. I expected a symmetrical interchange with a bridge across the freeway, and was halfway down the ramp before I saw it was freeway-only.

Fortunately, it was a sunny afternoon and traffic was light. I cautiously crossed the on-ramp to the paired off-ramp, waited for the big truck to zoom by, and biked back out of there.

I had noticed the street did not look bike-friendly as I turned onto it, and considered detouring to an easier route, but I thought I could tough it out and it would get easier later.

Internal on-ramps. The incident stayed with me as a metaphor for subtle triggering. Sometimes we believe we are safely out of reach of emergency mode, when we are already heading toward it. Our internal landscape can have surprisingly long on-ramps, with few opportunities to turn aside to an easier route.

One metaphorical on-ramp is the need to appear "normal" in stressful circumstances. "Everyone else" can handle a crowded grocery store, so we pretend everything is fine and keep shopping, which leads to feeling exhausted, overwhelmed, and panicky. An easier road might be to leave and come back later when it is less crowded.

Another metaphorical on-ramp is the need to be perfect. Any small mistake fuels a spiral of shame and despair. An easier road might be compassionate awareness that we all make mistakes, fix them as best we can, and continue on our way.

No easy solution. Sometimes it is not so simple to find an easier road. We may know that everyone makes mistakes, and at the same time a voice out of the past or the present says that mistakes are a threat to survival. In a double bind where any choice leads to punishment (or panic), a demand to find an easier road only leads to more stress. In this case, easier might mean acknowledging a dilemma and easing the pressure to find a solution. "I don't know what to do about this right now."

Permission for ease. We might have a voice out of the past or the present that says "easier" is lazy or bad. We hear, "Life is hard for everyone. Relationships are hard. Anything worth having is worth working for." While everyone encounters difficulties in life, there is a difference between putting in a lot of effort, and enduring excruciating pain.

Survivors of traumatic childhoods often take a high level of pain and effort for granted, and assume that life could be even harder than that. The first step toward an easier road might be permission to make choices that lessen pain.

We may believe that our worth is measured by how much we can achieve, and we need to work as hard as possible all the time, regardless of the cost, to deserve approval. In truth, we all deserve approval, whether we achieve everything or nothing or something in between, whether we are relaxing or struggling. One way to find an easier road might be to examine our standards for self-approval and change them over time.

Between easiest and hardest. What is easier for one person can harder for another. We tend to think that what is hard for us is easy for everyone else, and what is easy for us is also easy for everyone else, even if we worked for years to gain that skill. We can allow ourselves to turn toward what is easy for us, both our talents and our hard-won skills.

As we choose easier roads, we do not want to fall in with our culture's defaults, to reward and defer to people who are already in power, and ignore or oppress people who are already marginalized. Turning toward an easier road does not mean taking the easiest road. It does not mean ignoring values, ethics, and harm to others or ourselves. We can meander on our way between easiest and hardest, making choices in the moment that balance our inner and outer resources with the results we want to achieve.

Inner roadmap. On your inner roadmap, are you familiar with some long on-ramps to being triggered? Hours, days, or months after missing a crucial turning point, you might recognize the triggering events. Long on-ramps can be part of frustrating recurring patterns.

Already okay. Take some time to sit with the possibility of more ease in a troubling situation. How does the contemplation of more ease feel in your body? Do any dissenting voices arise? Say hello to anything and everything you experience.

After a generous amount of time with the possibility of ease, gently sense into what shape easier might take. It might be something you have known all along, or a bit of advice that comes floating back to you, or an entirely new idea. It might be an action, or a non-action, or a shift in how you view the situation or yourself. What if you have nothing to prove? What if you are already doing the right thing? What if, despite any and all evidence to the contrary, you are already okay?

Mark the trail. Sometimes we only find out what is easier after doing something the hard way, and the best we can do is mark the trail for the future. Several friends tell me they have inadvertently taken that same freeway on-ramp, both by bike and by car. I sent an email to the Traffic Safety department suggesting "Freeway Only" signs at that intersection, to make it easier for all of us, and they did add a new sign.

As we map out our changing inner landscapes, we can sometimes choose an easier road based on past experience. Most of the time, we can only choose the road that appears easier to our current perceptions. Above all, we can be gentle with ourselves no matter how our choices turn out.

Decision-Free Zone

Do you have a decision you're weighing or a dilemma that is causing you stress? A Decision-Free Zone is a safe time and space to listen to all of yourself, with a clear boundary that action is off the table. You can write in a journal, talk with a friend, or explore in a healing session.

As you listen for what is true for you in the moment without restrictions, you may discover conflicting emotions, underlying considerations, increasing uncertainty, or a calm knowledge about your next step. As you set aside your ideas about what a solution "should" look like, new ideas may float to the surface.

Allow uncertainty. The first step is to acknowledge uncertainty. At this moment, you do not have clarity about the best answer. Can you allow yourself to feel uncertain? We often judge ourselves for not yet knowing what we want, especially if we think there is one right answer we "should" find.

Sometimes there is no best answer to a complex situation. Several choices are equally good, or equally bad, or too different to compare.

The future is unknown. Sometimes a decision hinges on guessing the future. We can twist ourselves into knots trying to guess, or holding ourselves responsible for guesses that turned out to be wrong. How does it feel to absolve yourself of responsibility for predicting the future?

Put action on hold. After we allow uncertainty and our

lack of knowledge about the future, we can make space for what we do know to emerge. Often we push away emotions, thoughts, memories, and intuition because we do not like where they lead.

- If I feel angry, I have to leave him.
- If I acknowledge discomfort with my gender, I have to take hormones.
- If I think it's a good career move, I have to accept this job.
- If I miss her, I have to get in touch.

None of those conclusions are true. You can connect with emotions, thoughts, memories, and intuition and sit with them, letting them be themselves. They do not remove your power of choice, and in fact may reveal more choices as you wait and listen.

Keisha's dilemma. Keisha examines the swelling on her wrist worriedly. She has debated making a doctor's appointment for a week already. She cannot decide, even when she acknowledges that she cannot guess whether the swelling is serious or not.

When she takes some decision-free time to be with herself and her emotions, shame and anger rise to the surface. Despite her employer's good medical insurance and Keisha's careful attention to appearance, her doctor's receptionist quizzes her repeatedly about her ability to pay. Keisha's shoulders slump as she tells herself it is probably coincidence, nothing to do with her dark skin and natural hair, and she should be grateful to have access to medical care.

As she continues to pay attention to what is true for her, she remembers that she has never seen even raggedly dressed white patients stand at the receptionist's window as long as she does. Her refusal to be quizzed again crystallizes. Her shoulders straighten with relief as she connects with her right to respectful treatment no matter what her appearance.

Now that she understands her hesitation, she can separate her desire for medical care from the receptionist's racist behavior. New ideas arise. She briefly considers writing a letter to her doctor, but feels her shoulders tense again. She could find a doctor with more respectful staff. When she thinks of asking friends for recommendations, she feels light and clear.

Change the question. The decision-free time widened Keisha's question from, "Should I call my doctor about my wrist?" to "Do I want a new doctor?" It also highlighted the way her Inner Critic added to her confusion by questioning her observations and intuition.

Compassion for indecision. Like other creative processes, decision-making takes you into the unknown one step at a time. Whether you are sitting with a hard decision now or looking back at decisions that you regret, bring in as much compassion as you can. In each moment, you are making the best decisions you can with the information you have available.

Navigate Change: Mind the Gap

When we reach a decision and step forward into an inviting future, we need to pay attention to the gap between our existing habits and our changed environment. If a change is unwanted or the future is uncertain, we have even more reasons to be mindful during a transition. When we choose to heal, we invite ongoing change into our lives.

Transitions are hard. "Soon it will be time to put the toys away and wash your hands for dinner." "In five minutes we'll start putting your toys away." "Which toy would you like to put away first?"

If a parent tries to move a small child abruptly from one activity to another, a loud, tearful protest is the likely outcome. If the child gets several chances to get used to the idea, the transition proceeds more smoothly.

As we grow older, most of us lose our tendency to protest loudly and tearfully in public, but we continue to dislike abrupt change. We want to know what to expect and how to handle it.

Trauma adds anxiety. Unexpected change naturally irritates the nervous system and triggers anxiety. In a system already braced for danger, change is interpreted as threatening to a fragile sense of control and safety.

Daily transitions. As you move through your day, do you ease slowly from one activity to another, or shift quickly? What resources help you navigate daily transitions? You might see some of your habits in a new light. Some examples:

- Take a deep breath
- Have a hot drink or a snack
- Stand and stretch
- Sit and rest
- Check for new messages
- Complete a task
- Leave a task unfinished as a starting point for next time.

Does your day contain any rough transitions that leave you edgy and unsettled? What can you add to give your nervous system more time to adjust to the change?

Life transitions. Our bodies relax into familiarity, even if we long for change. Muscle memory carries us efficiently through routines worn smooth by repetition and optimized by small changes over time.

Whether a life transition is sudden or planned, traumatic or happy, it inevitably disrupts our routines. Our muscle memory no longer applies, requiring us to learn new patterns of movement with conscious attention. We make confused, awkward mistakes despite our best efforts. Time moves more slowly as we concentrate. We feel anxious, frustrated, and overwhelmed by the flood of new information.

Make allowances. Give yourself time to adapt, explore, and not yet know the answers. In a month, you will have established new habits. For now, you are a beginner. What judgments or preconceptions do you have about adult beginners? What are your thoughts, feelings, and experiences as a beginner in this moment?

Build in time to breathe, rest, and replenish your energy.

Are there any commitments you can put aside until the adjustment period is past? Allow anxiety, frustration, and other difficult feelings to move through you like a wave.

Manage uncertainty. Sometimes there is an uncomfortably long hallway between an old door closing and a new door opening. The extended gap challenges us to manage uncertainty while we create a new future out of the unknown one step at a time. What judgments and preconceptions do you have about uncertainty?

Rather than rush through the period of uncertainty, acknowledge and experience it fully. Even though we prefer certainty and stability, there can be a spaciousness in not-knowing. What is your physical experience of uncertainty? What can you enjoy about it?

Ask for support. As isolating as uncertainty can be, you are not the first nor the last to struggle with it. No matter how you reached this point, blame will not help you. Ask for understanding and support from the people around you. As much as you can, bring compassion to your experience and the ways you respond to it. Seek out nourishment for your spirit in this in-between time. Simple meditation can help you stay connected to your self.

Space for healing. The process of healing is a commitment to change, and at the same time a commitment to acceptance of our truth in each moment. When we move mindfully through small and large gaps, we create space in our lives for healing.

All Done! Tools for Rapid Change

At her first appointment, Kyung describes unrelenting anxiety that interferes with eating, sleeping, working, and enjoying life. "I'm done! I've tried Rescue Remedy, meditation, therapy, and meds. I need it to stop now!"

While I might be tempted to explain that most change is slow and gradual, the energy of "Done!" can herald big shifts. Together we pay attention to the details of what is happening in her body.

Tool: Allow space for everything. One powerful tool for change is to allow space for everything that is present. Be with the need for change, sense into its urgency and complexity, and validate being done with "reasonable" and "moderate". Be with the symptoms you want to change as well. They both make sense in their own contexts.

Kyung says hello to her anxiety as she feels it in this moment, and also says hello to the urgent need for the anxiety to stop. She feels anxiety off to her left, and "all done" to her right, with room for both of them to be there at the same time. We let them both know they can be exactly the way they are for as long as they want. She sighs with relief as some of the pressure eases.

Tool: Drop what is not yours. When we try everything to solve a problem, and nothing works, we tend to believe we are not trying hard enough. We work harder, faster, longer until we exhaust our resources. The "All done!" of exhaustion breaks that cycle, allowing us to consider that the problem might not be ours at all.

We have no leverage on energy that is not ours. When we try to change ourselves to fix a problem we did not cause, we only dig the hole deeper, until we finally put down the shovel and realize we were okay all along.

As Kyung sits with both her anxiety and the need for it to stop, she thinks of her grandmother, who lived with them when she was small. With adult perspective, she recognizes her grandmother's anxious mannerisms, and her own loving wish to soothe the tension. As she considers whether some of her anxiety might belong to her grandmother, she feels a heavy burden lift away and laughs, astonished.

Dropping what is not ours brings change simply and quickly. The catch is that we have to accept the feelings first. As long as we resist, we cannot let go. After we surrender to the truth of our experience, wondering "Maybe this isn't mine," can bring lightness and ease.

Trust in recycling. When we feel overwhelmed, chaotic, and trapped, we might have recently picked up others' energy. Clearing it away puts us back in contact with inner calm. We can gently brush our hands along the body, sweeping away energy that no longer serves us.

Sometimes we hold on to what is not ours because we want to protect the people around us from harmful energy. We might also worry about how to push the energy back to its rightful owner. I visualize an energy shower from the ceiling, flowing toward a drain in the floor. Any released energy gets carried into to the earth for recycling. Where it goes after that is not our problem nor our business.

Listen for "Let it go!" Sometimes we advise ourselves, "Let it go!" Say hello to that voice, and listen for what it does not want. It might not want a fight, or internal distress, or to appear obsessive or attached. Beneath that, listen for what it does want: perhaps peace, or calm, or balance. Also listen for what is being admonished to let go. Somewhere, something is holding on, or feeling an internally disallowed emotion like anger or shame. Consider making room for both parts to be just the way they are for as long as they want.

Feeling done with life. Sometimes "All done!" with an intolerably painful situation can manifest as suicidal thoughts, or feeling done with life. Intense shame can also lead to suicidal thoughts.

The first priority is to stay safe. If you have a suicidal plan, please remember that you can gain new tools to manage and alleviate pain*. When feeling done with life, create a lot of space for what is true right now, including wanting to die, wanting to live, and the reactions to all of that. Allow anything that is not yours to fall away. In particular, shame that belongs to abusers seems to stick to their victims instead. Send that shame into to the earth!

Decisions and risks. "All done!" might apply to a job, career, housing situation, or relationship with ups and downs, where the latest boundary violation has tipped the balance from "workable" to "no more." The shift might be a surprise, or it might be the culmination of a long struggle for resolution. A solid sense of being done opens doors to risks and decisions that were previously unpalatable.

"All done!" might also mark withdrawal from a level of risk or uncertainty that is now unacceptable after yet another red flag. A self-protective instinct from deep inside demands change from existing patterns. Asking for help

---

* metanoia.org/suicide/ offers compassionate, practical encouragement to stay alive.

might become a new possibility for one person, while another person might go it alone for the first time.

Tool: Already solved. How would it feel if the issue changed right now? Is there something inside that is already there? Does anything object to the new feeling? Hidden resistance might come forward in response to imagined success. Listen for its truth.

Alternatively, imagining success might show a clear path to reach it. Ask inside, "What if this problem is already solved?" Open to words, images, and emotions that carry a new solution. Perhaps a switch can shut off the emergency alarm triggered long ago, and anxiety can just stop.

Emerge into new terrain. Like Kyung, we may have struggled with a recurring issue for years, full of frustration and despair, until the clarity or surprise of "All done!" brings a shift. When we allow all our conflicting feelings to be present, drop what is not ours, and imagine the problem is already solved, we can emerge into new terrain.

Check In With Your Chakras

We can shift our perspective, bring attention to areas we usually ignore, and find more balance by paying attention to our energy systems as they are in the present moment.

The chakras are energy centers along the front of the spine from tailbone to crown. They are a key part of the energy map of the human body, developed around 3,000 years ago in India. Some people dedicate years of focused yoga and other meditative practices to refine the connection between body and mind, allowing energy to flow freely through the chakras, leading to kundalini awakening and enlightenment.

Chakras are associated with a rainbow of colors and symbols, although each person's experience of their own chakras varies. Energy moves through the system from bottom to top in a "liberating" current, and from top to bottom in a "manifesting" current. The type of energy associated with the chakras ranges from solid matter at the first chakra to pure awareness at the seventh.

Individual energies. As you read the description of each chakra, sense gently into its location. You might sense a traditional spinning energy center, or a more vague sense of flow or blockage, or bright colors, or sounds, or emotions. Anything you sense is right for you. Each chakra might be tightly closed, balanced and flowing, or locked open.

Notice what feels easy about each kind of energy, and what feels hard. Even if that part of your life seems to be in complete disarray, there is still a spark of that energy in you. For example, the first chakra is associated with survival. Even if your survival seems in doubt at each moment, there is still something in you fighting to live, since you are still here.

Trauma affects all the chakras. The chakra system helps us focus on one kind of healing at a time, and notice what is going well in addition to what is difficult.

Root Chakra, Muladhara (root support), "I am." The first chakra relates to survival, physical embodiment, family, and grounding. Through our legs and our sit bones, we physically connect to the earth. Sense for this chakra at the perineum, or the tip of the tailbone. You can also visualize it filling the whole bowl of the pelvis.

Trauma divides us from our bodies. Early abuse makes us question our fundamental right to be here. Rather than being a source of safety and support, family becomes a source of struggle and pain. As we heal from trauma, we treasure each regained scrap of physical awareness. We sense our determination to survive as we battle with despair.

Sacral Chakra, Svadhisthana (sweetness, one's own abode), "I want." The second chakra relates to gestation, sexuality, desire, and pleasure. Sense for this chakra at the level of the sacrum, or womb for those who have one. It can overlap with the first chakra.

Sexual abuse causes this chakra to shut down, or get locked open. We question our right to want. We question our right to allow desires and ideas to develop in quiet darkness until our own sense of timing says they are ripe to be born. As we heal, we learn patience with our deep rhythms.

Solar Plexus Chakra, Manipura (lustrous gem), "I will." The third chakra relates to power, will, assertiveness, and boundaries. Sense for this chakra behind the navel, at the solar plexus.

Abuse and trauma teach us about helplessness and power-over, rather than strength and power-within. As we heal, we learn to take back our power and take action on our own behalf.

Heart Chakra, Anahata (unstruck, fresh), "I love." The fourth chakra relates to love, connection, and compassion. Through our arms we reach out to the world around us. As the center of the chakra system, it also relates to centering and balance. Sense for this chakra in your heart and chest.

Child abuse and partner abuse mix our natural wellspring of love with pain and shame. As we heal, we learn that love does not have to hurt, and we regain compassion for ourselves as well as others. Over time, tightly closed hearts can open again, and wide-open hearts can learn self-protection. Rather than looking for the one right way, we weave a middle way between extremes.

Throat Chakra, Visuddha (purification), "I speak." The fifth chakra relates to speech, expression, and communication. Sense for this chakra in your neck and throat, connecting down toward your collarbones and up toward your mouth.

Many abusers explicitly silence their victims with threats, lies, and coercion. Society implicitly silences survivors with disbelief, victim-blaming, and lack of attention. Fear and shame strangle our voices. As we heal, we allow our truth to resonate freely inside our bodies and ring out in the world.

Third Eye Chakra, Ajna (perceive), "I see." The sixth chakra relates to vision, perception, and intuition. Sense for this chakra between your eyes, behind your forehead.

Trauma leads to hypervigilance, straining to see every

possible threat and sense every nuance of the environment. Trauma also narrows our visual field, focusing on one thing at a time. Abuse often includes gaslighting, intentional questioning of our perceptions. As we heal, we can relax our eyes (and the rest of the body), allowing information to come to us rather than straining toward it. Our visual field can expand and soften when we no longer feel threatened. Gently covering our eyes with the palms of our hands can give them a rest.

Crown Chakra, Sahasrara (thousand-fold), "I know." The seventh chakra connects us with All That Is. Where the first chakra is the most embodied, personal, individual chakra, the seventh is the most universal, spiritual, blended one. Sense for this chakra at the crown of your head.

Spiritual abuse directly damages our connection to Spirit. Trauma divides us from ourselves, and from the rest of the world. We wonder why we were harmed, and if we somehow deserved it. As we heal, we realize that no one deserves trauma, and we are all interconnected.

Your whole system. Now that you have been introduced to each chakra, check in with your system as a whole. As you sit or lie down, invite each part of your spine to relax into support, starting from your tailbone and moving up through each section to the top of your head. Do any areas feel cluttered, snagged, blocked, or overwhelmed? What parts of the system feel clear and flowing? How do they relate to each other?

Can you allow earth energy to rise through your system through the root chakra? Can you allow spiritual energy to flow down through the crown chakra? You could bring a gentle hand to any uncomfortable areas. Invite any energy that does not belong to you, or no longer serves you, to flow away, to be recycled in the earth. You could also invite areas with more energy to support areas with less.

Respect for your balance. Each body has its own sense of balance and rightness, with some chakras more open that others. Consider offering respect for the way your system has managed the energies and events of your life. As you heal, your system responds to present conditions in a flexible, connected way.

Weave Your Body Whole

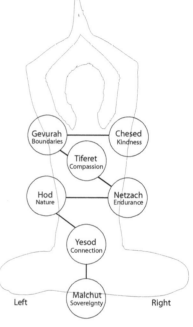

Jewish Kabbalah gives us another view of energy systems in the body.

Trauma fractures us internally and externally, splitting our sense of our bodies and sundering our connections with the rest of the world. Counting days with Jewish Kabbalah can help us weave ourselves back together, looking at qualities of kindness, boundaries, compassion, endurance, Nature, connection, and sovereignty.

Any tool can harm as well as heal. Kabbalah in particular has been co-opted to gather and steal power over others, instead of supporting personal power within as it was intended. Jewish Kabbalah can be religious, mystical, intellectual, esoteric. My focus here is body awareness to restore internal and external connections.

Tree of Life. The Kabbalistic Tree of Life has 10 energy centers, called sefirot (singular, sefira, "seh-fee-rah"). Like the chakras, the one at the head is most universal and spiritual, and they become more specific and material as they go down the body. Unlike the chakras, they are not all on the body's centerline.

The top three sefirot, Keter at the crown of the head and Hochma and Binah on either side of it, are considered too subtle for us to sense. The process of "counting the omer" (counting the 49 days from Passover to Shavuot*) focuses on the lower seven, as pictured.

Weave a sefira with the others. Choose a sefira, perhaps the one you are most comfortable with, as your focus for a week. Pair it with each sefira in the order given below from Chesed/kindness to Malchut/sovereignty, one on each day for seven days.

For example, if you choose the first sefira Chesed/kindness as your focus, the first day it will pair with itself. The second day focuses on Gevurah/boundaries, in the context of Chesed. Can you allow kindness to bathe your boundaries?

Each person finds their own images and meanings for the pairings. Matching our perceptions and the events of our lives with the day's theme can lead to surprising insights.

The full process of counting the omer focuses on each sefira in turn over seven weeks. This slow weaving of each sefira to all the others shows us which are comfortable and familiar, which we wrestle with, and which are unexplored enigmas.

Sefira of the week and day. Each evening after sundown, read a little bit about the following day's pairing. I used Susan Windle's intimate memoir of counting the omer, *Through the Gates*, as a primary source, and read other

---

* See jewfaq.org/holidayb.htm for more about the Jewish tradition of counting the omer.

sources as well.

Sense into your body for the location of this week's sefira, and then into the location for this day's sefira. Can you connect them to each other? Do they feel vividly alive, or remote, or numb, or something else? Do you have chronic pain or remembered trauma there? What strength and capability do you find there?

How do you relate to the meaning of the day's sefira, in the context of the week's sefira? What interpretations resonate in your life? What emotions arise in response? Accept whatever happens in that day as part of the process.

Chesed: love, kindness, grace, benevolence. Chesed, in the right shoulder, is where the energy of Spirit becomes tangible to us as a flood of loving, accepting energy.

While this sounds warm and fuzzy, what I experienced in my right shoulder was chronic pain and restriction. When I tried to connect with the energy of this sefira, I felt anger and grief. At first I assumed the process was not working for me. When I accepted what I was sensing, it felt healing that Spirit could respond with sympathetic anger and grief to injustice and pain. I felt a shift around having protection, and being worthy of protection.

Trauma often damages our relationship to Spirit. Part of being embodied is sensing that we are securely part of the world, wanted and important. Notice how it feels to bring that energy to each of the other sefirot over the first week. Resistance, conflict, and contradictory messages are all part of this process.

Gevurah: strength, justice, limits, boundaries. Gevurah, in the left shoulder, represents limits of tangible form, where the previous sefirot are all about the potential of limitless energy. While this sefira is often seen in a negative light, I think judgments, tangible limits, and boundaries are tremendously positive. While it might be fun to be a boundless energy being, we cannot be embodied without edges. Notice how it feels to offer each sefira strength and boundaries, like the banks of a river.

Tiferet: beauty, harmony, balance, compassion. Located at the heart, forming the center-point of the Tree of Life, Tiferet represents inner beauty, balance, and compassion. While Chesed represents our connection with an endless flow of loving energy, Tiferet is our own capacity for acceptance and compassion. I noticed that while I have a lot of practice extending this energy to others, I find it harder to offer to myself.

Notice how it feels to bring compassion and look for the beauty in each sefira in turn. When Tiferet met Yesod, I understood at a deeper level that my body is allowed to want. Acceptance of wanting is an essential part of accepting being alive.

Netzach: endurance, victory, physical energy, persistence. At the right side of the solar plexus, Netzach represents endurance, a familiar force in my life. I have been known as "stubborn" since I was small. Surviving trauma, and the aftermath of trauma, requires a lot of endurance.

How does endurance and persistence manifest in your life? What are you enduring, physically and emotionally? What are you persistent about in relation to each sefira?

Hod: splendor, humility, glory of Nature. At the left side of the solar plexus, Hod represents the humble splendor of the physical world. One source related this sefira to perception, which resonated for me. As each sefira supported my perceptions, it felt like a whole week of anti-gaslighting.

What do you notice around being embodied in the natural

world, in relation to each of the sefirot? Can you spend some time outside this week?

Yesod: intimacy, foundation, connections. At the level of the sacrum, or womb for those who have one, Yesod represents intimacy, relationships, wanting, the foundation of being alive and embodied.

Many trauma survivors are disconnected from the whole pelvic area, and this is an opportunity to reconnect. It can bring a flood of emotions: longing for intimacy and connection, grief for lost connections, fear of the primal desires of the body, and anger about the assaults this area may have endured. It can also bring up pain around community and abuse, including "Why didn't anyone help?"

For me, this was the hardest week, and at the same time it brought the biggest changes in how I relate to my body. Instead of feeling my pelvic area as "that, over there," I feel it as "right here, part of me." How does your pelvic area relate to each of the other sefirot?

Malchut: leadership, sovereignty, integrity. Below the pelvis, or at the feet, or the whole of you, Malchut represents your sovereignty over yourself, and grounded leadership. For me, the week of Malchut was about integrating the prior week's changes around Yesod. I also noticed a quiet pride and confidence in my style of collaborative leadership.

How does it feel to integrate each sefira into the whole of you? How do you see yourself as a leader in each area?

Wholeness. However much we might hope that healing will turn us into someone else, we find wholeness in becoming more ourselves. As we weave the bits of ourselves back together, we leave behind the isolation of trauma for a more secure and connected place in the world.

Resources

Robyn Posin's *Go Only As Fast As Your Slowest Part Feels Safe To Go: Tales to Kindle Gentleness and Compassion for Our Exhausted Selves*, Compassionate Ink, 2013, shares her discoveries about slowness and healing.

Crash Course: A Self Healing Guide to Auto Accident Trauma & Recovery, North Atlantic Books, 2001, by Diane Poole Heller gives practical, gentle instructions on applying Somatic Experiencing to car crashes. The exercises can easily be applied to other acute traumas.

Overcoming Trauma Through Yoga: Reclaiming Your Body, North Atlantic Books, 2011, by David Emerson and Elizabeth Hopper compassionately describes trauma-aware yoga, including choices to make poses easier and permission to stop doing anything that causes pain.

Christopher Germer's *The Mindful Path to Self-Compassion: Freeing Yourself from Destructive Thoughts and Emotions*, Guilford Publications, 2009 offers many tools for sitting with our struggles and dilemmas.

How to Get From Where You Are to Where You Want to Be, Hay House, 2000, by Cheri Huber contains stories and advice about being with your experience, no matter how hard it is.

Anodea Judith's *Wheels of Life: A Users Guide to the Chakra System*, Llewellyn Publications, 1999, provides a thorough, inclusive introduction to the chakra system.

Susan Windle's intimate memoir of counting the omer, *Through the Gates: A Practice for Counting the Omer*, CreateSpace, 2014, is a great feminist resource for learning about Kabbalah.

Presence After Trauma

2: Acceptance

Some people think of acceptance as the end goal of a healing process, an achievement of spiritual non-attachment.

I think of acceptance as a daily companion, a healing tool that applies at each stage of the process, from first accepting that trauma occurred, to accepting its current effects on us, to accepting ourselves just as we are. Acceptance is saying hello to all aspects of our present experience, including the parts we hate and the parts we are ashamed of and the confused muddle we cannot even sort out into parts.

Simple but not easy, acceptance acknowledges, "This is how it is right now." Acceptance allows anything, including the demand for things to be different. It is not always spacious, compassionate, warm. Even grudging, tentative, last resort acceptance often brings a breath of relief, a little extra room for movement, or rest.

Acceptance lays the groundwork for both reconciling with ourselves and reconciling with the world. We can send approval back to a younger self, accept shadow aspects of ourselves, and give up on the quest to be "normal." We can take a break from healing, and accept that we will not always reach our goals. We can accept that we never deserved abuse, and yet it happened. We can know that we were always worthy of protection, and gradually acknowledge and integrate split-off parts of ourselves.

Achieve Approval

Trauma interrupts life's narrative and bends its trajectory, challenging the illusion that our choices control every outcome. Mainstream society responds with victim-blaming, "You must have done something to cause it," and continues with isolation and disapproval. "You don't fit in well enough."

Instead of compassion, survivors receive subtle or overt messages about not measuring up, not getting better fast enough, and not fitting the narrative of a competent adult. Our cultural myths of independence and imperviousness lead to harsh judgment of people who are overwhelmed by traumatic events.

Survivors' energy that might be used to fit in is devoted to recovery and healing instead. There is less energy available to maintain social masks, while triggers and sensitivities require setting boundaries rather than going along with the flow.

Longing is allowed. We have a myth that adults "should" be self-validating, with no need for outside approval. In truth, we all share the need to see ourselves reflected in loving eyes. We depend on society not only for physical survival, but also for emotional connection and reassurance. Social isolation is doubly painful to those who already feel damaged by trauma.

Is there a longing for approval inside you, buried under the "shoulds"? To acknowledge it without feeling overwhelmed, you can say, "Something in me feels a longing for approval, and I say hello to that." Take some time to acknowledge all your responses around the topic of approval. Your Inner Critic may have a lot to say.

Do you long for approval from a specific source? The judgments of a critical parent or teacher can continue to echo long after the person loses power over your daily life. You might long for spiritual assurance that you are a good person. You might want present-day approval of your labors from the people around you.

Approved right now. Imagine that your desired source approves of you right now. This person, this being, is filled with radiant love, approval, and pleasure at your very existence. Nothing could possibly shake this person's good opinion of you. This being's regard is large enough and positive enough to encompass every truth of your past and present.

Soak in it like a hot tub, like sunshine, like spring rain. Let it nourish each individual cell. Notice your physical and emotional responses to approval.

Approval across time. What trickles or floods of approval do you remember receiving over time? Your Inner Nurturer gathers those memories to support you. What parts of yourself can you whole-heartedly approve of?

As we learn and grow, we sometimes look back at younger selves with critical eyes. Think about your struggles and triumphs five years ago, and send back approval and respect for yourself-then. Take time to visualize yourself as a young adult, a teen, a young child, and an infant. Remember what each younger self accomplished and what obstacles they faced. What doors did they open for you? Send back approval to each of those selves.

Imagine that an older, wiser self from five years in the future sends approval back to you now. Notice how that feels in your body. What are you working on now that your future self will appreciate? You have always done the best you could with the resources you had. You were born approved, and no action or trauma can make you deserve anything less than approval.

Belong to the club. In abusive situations, approval depends on pleasing the person in power. Authentic selves are kept carefully hidden, protected from shaming or punishment. During healing, authenticity becomes a higher priority, and yet the habit of seeking approval persists. We imagine a secret club of people who are healed enough, and work hard to deserve membership.

After many years, we look around and realize this club has no officers or rules. Each person claims membership for themselves. Consider joining!

Unhook from Projection

As we grow up, we learn that some qualities bring us more approval and acceptance than others.

Beatrice's reaction to hearing, "You're controlling!" depends on her beliefs and assumptions. If she believes that controlling people are abusive and bad, she will react defensively, at least in the privacy of her mind.

- I am not!
- No, you are!
- I don't like you.
- If you think I'm controlling, there's something wrong with me.

On the other hand, if she believes that everyone is controlling sometimes, she can respond calmly to the immediate content of the statement. "My friend Tomás thinks I behaved in a controlling way."

All qualities. We each contain the potential for all qualities, ranging from wonderful to terrible. When you think back, you can probably remember times when you have been controlling and yielding, cruel and kind, greedy and generous.

Pushed into shadow. We start out freely expressing all of ourselves, but quickly learn that some qualities are rewarded more than others. We emphasize the qualities that get us what we want, and push away qualities that are frowned on or punished. The qualities we push away, both positive and negative, accumulate into our shadow.

What qualities live in your shadow? Quickly complete these phrases:

- Only bad people _____
- I hate it when people _____
- I would never be _____
- I wish I were _____
- This person is my hero because _____

When we despise or long for a quality, we contain enough of it to recognize it. Other people's actions catch on the hooks inside us and provoke strong reactions. When we acknowledge our shadow qualities, the hooks are smoothed away, and we can observe without reacting.

When we acknowledge our capacity for a full range of behaviors, we can choose appropriately for each situation. When we limit ourselves to a narrow range, we have fewer conscious options, and our shadow expresses itself without our awareness.

Projected outward. Projection is assigning those unwanted qualities to the people around us instead of acknowledging them within ourselves. We think everyone else should work as hard as we do to keep the same qualities squashed, and react strongly to small signs of them. This leads to conflict, since we each have a unique set of qualities in our shadow.

When we believe only bad people are controlling, we work hard not to be controlling, deny that we are ever controlling (or hate ourselves for it), and judge others harshly for being controlling. We spend a lot of energy fighting with a quality we want to avoid.

How to unhook. Beatrice notices that being controlling has come up a lot lately. A surprising number of people are trying to control her, or accuse her of being controlling. She decides to take a look at her relationship with control.

- **Notice.** She brings the incidents around control into her awareness.
- **Own it.** She repeats "I am controlling," and looks compassionately for times when this has been true. She realizes that when she is concerned about safety, she tries to control other people. She also harshly controls herself to be "good." She sits with grief and shame, breathing through the strong emotions until they pass.
- **Beliefs.** She looks at her beliefs around being controlling, and their origins. She remembers struggling against other people's control in the past, and learning that controlling others is disrespectful. She looks at all the times she was taught she was bad, and needed to control herself for approval.
- **Benefits.** She looks at the benefits of being controlling. Taking control of herself and her environment supports her boundaries and makes it less likely that someone else will inappropriately take control of her life.

Inner change. If Beatrice has projected "controlling" onto events that are not about her, unhooking from her projections will dramatically change her experience. Perhaps Tomás only teased her about speaking assertively, and does not think she is controlling at all. Usually, events are not a neutral background, and change comes more slowly. Beatrice might look back over months or years of work and realize that control no longer comes up as much.

If she notices herself being inappropriately controlling in

the present, she can apologize, make amends, and work to change her behavior.

External response. Now that Beatrice fully acknowledges her capacity for control, she can also discern clearly when she has not been controlling. If Tomás accuses her again, she might notice that he also has issues with control.

It is rarely effective to tell someone, "You're projecting!" Mutual accusations of projection create a hall of mirrors where the truth is lost in distorting reflections. A neutral question, "What makes you say that?" gives Tomás the opportunity to check his assumptions.

Not the problem. Like most powerful tools, unhooking from projection can be misused. The most common misuse is to assume it will change the outside world, and that a lack of immediate change means we need to work harder. When we own our projections, we change our perception of the world and how we interact with it. While it can be comforting to believe that we control everything that happens to us, most of us do not have that kind of privilege and power.

If unhooking from a projection has no effect, it means we are probably not the one creating the problem. That information can free us to look for other solutions, such as expressing boundaries or leaving the situation.

Accusations and gaslighting. Accusations of projection can be used to gaslight, casting doubt on people's perceptions. For example, present-time abusers accuse survivors of projecting old memories when survivors confront abusive actions. Vulnerable survivors are already accustomed to believing others instead of their own perceptions, especially when awash in flashbacks.

A powerful antidote is to own projection itself. A survivor can work through the process and say, "Yes, I project sometimes." If acknowledging projection does not change the situation, then projection is not the only problem.

Fallible and clear. When we unhook from projections, we acknowledge that we are fallible, opening the door to compassion for ourselves and others. No one is perfectly good or perfectly bad. When we stop fighting our shadows, we see ourselves and the rest of the world more clearly. The energy we put into condemnation becomes available for enjoyment instead.

The Tyranny of Normal

A big part of healing is to discover and accept the unique version of "normal" for each of us, instead of stuffing anything that does not seem normal into our shadows.

When first remembering childhood abuse, many survivors mourn the loss of a "normal" past. Mainstream media sells us a vision of what our lives should be, and convinces us we are less-than if our lives are different. Even if we live in a home that embraces difference, we may feel shame when we venture outside. At the same time, survivors may accept violence as a "normal" part of family life, never having known anything else.

Violence is common. Survivors of violence feel alienated, cut off from normal experience. In part, that comes from dissociation, feeling separate from the physical experience of being alive. In part, it comes from society's myth that experiencing violence is rare and abnormal.

Abuse is heartbreakingly common. In the United States, at least 1 in 4 girls and 1 in 6 boys are sexually assaulted by age 18.* Intimate partner violence is endemic.** The same mainstream media that idolizes childhood innocence is full

---

* National Association of Adult Survivors of Child Abuse (NAASCA) – What are the statistics of the abused? www.naasca. org/2012-Resources/010812-StaisticsOfChildAbuse.htm

** Centers for Disease Control and Prevention (CDC) – The National Intimate Partner and Sexual Violence Survey. www.cdc. gov/violenceprevention/nisvs/index.html

of overt violence.

We send soldiers into war zones to both commit and suffer atrocities, and then tell them their experiences are "inhuman" when they return. Humans clearly commit and experience violence at high rates, so we cannot claim that war is outside the realm of "normal" human experience.

Normal is relative. The dictionary defines normal as "usual, ordinary". Each of us defines "usual" and "ordinary" based on our viewpoint and environment. Small children stare, point, and comment when they encounter something new to them, such as a person using a wheelchair.

The wiktionary entry also notes*:

> *"Warning: normal, when used to describe a majority group of people, can be considered offensive to those who don't consider membership of their own minority to be unusual. Care should be taken when juxtaposing normal, particularly with stereotypical labels, to avoid undue insult."*

When applied to a majority group, "normal" supports the privilege of being the expected, accommodated default, while everyone else has to fit in around the edges.

Ideally, responsible adults teach children that "normal" is relative, and that it is good manners to be respectful as well as curious as they learn about what is normal for someone else. Sadly, many adults never learned this lesson themselves, moving through the world as if they are entitled to make others uncomfortable with their prying questions.

Avoid prying questions. When we ask questions to satisfy our curiosity, rather than to connect with someone, we are labeling them as Other, and demanding their time to

---

* en.wiktionary.org/wiki/normal

educate us. When we feel curious, we can pause to acknowledge that each person is normal to themselves before entering into conversation. We can also pay attention to people's responses, and stop asking if they seem uncomfortable.

Disability of any sort elicits the same rude questions over and over. United States culture encourages us to think we are entitled to intimate health details about anyone who appears different. Strangers are visibly taken aback when I decline to discuss the details of my sensitivities with them.

When the questions are directed at a disabled person's caregiver, the caregiver can say, "Ask them!" As the person being asked, we can say, "I'm not interested in discussing that further," or, "Nice weather we're having!" or calmly wait for them to find another topic.

When we realize that we have treated someone as Other, we might feel intense shame. We can apologize to the person and process our reaction elsewhere. We are all learning to be more aware and respectful of people who differ from what we assume is normal.

Your body is normal. Human bodies vary widely in size, shape, and other physical characteristics. Each body is normal in relation to itself, despite the myths we persist in believing against all evidence.

Myth: "Normal" weight is healthiest.

Fact: "Overweight" people have a lower risk of mortality than people of "normal" weight.*

---

* Time Magazine – Being Overweight Is Linked to Lower Risk of Mortality. healthland.time.com/2013/01/02/being-overweight-is-linked-to-lower-risk-of-mortality/

Myth: Human races are genetically different from each other.

Fact: Differences within races are larger than between races.*

Myth: Men and women are easy to distinguish from each other.

Fact: Differences within genders are larger than between genders.**

In the United States, whiteness and maleness are the default against which others are measured. The social costs of being considered less than "normal" account for a lot of the different outcomes between people of varying body sizes, skin colors, and genders.

PTSD is sensible. The dictionary also defines normal as "healthy; not sick or ill". As if the pain of trauma were not enough, survivors with PTSD feel additional pain at being considered abnormal. PTSD is the body's normal, sensible response to overwhelming trauma.

Normal for you. In what ways do you see yourself as normal? In what ways do you see yourself as less than or more than normal? Spend some time with your answers, with as much kindness and compassion as you can. Carry the questions inside as you interact with others who have their own sense of normalcy. Do your answers shift over time?

---

* PBS – RACE The Power of an Illusion background reading. www.pbs.org/race/000_About/002_04-background-01-02.htm

** American Psychological Association (APA) – Men and Women: No Big Difference. www.apa.org/research/action/difference.aspx

Take a Break from Healing

Have you thought about the finish line of your healing process? What would it take to declare yourself healed? What conscious and subconscious standards do you set for self-approval and time to rest in the present?

Do you compare your insides to other people's outsides? It is easy to believe that we have to keep our living space perfectly clean or never get triggered to consider ourselves healed. A common belief is that no one will violate our boundaries when we are healed enough.

Life is messier than that. Most people clean house just before someone comes over, so we all think everyone else's home is neater than ours. People do their best to conceal when they get triggered as well, so we believe we get triggered a lot more often than everyone else.

It is a toxic myth that if our boundaries are clear and strong enough, no one will violate them or hurt us. People's hurtful behavior is their choice. If we believe we are causing it somehow, we can change our behavior and see if their behavior changes in response. You do not have to be perfect to be treated with respect.

Rhythm of effort and rest. Healing is a long term process with times of effort and times of rest. There are frustrating plateaus where ongoing struggle yields little progress, then sudden breakthroughs to a new level. There are times of calm, joy, and harmony which we tend to attribute to our new skills and insights. There are times of catastrophe, loss, and defeat, which we tend to attribute to our brokenness. Life has a rhythm of change and consolidation for everyone, including times of feeling stuck without movement. Sometimes, breakthroughs to a new level are accompanied by the loss of everything that no longer fits. **Flexibility in the present.** Past trauma weaves through these patterns and affects them, but does not cause them. Being healed does not mean we have perfect control over our perfect circumstances. Healing is a process where gradually less of ourselves is frozen in the past, giving us more presence and flexibility to respond to our changing lives.

A lot of healing is about allowing ourselves to remember and come to accept uncomfortable truths. It can be scary to be involved in a healing process with unclear signs of progress toward urgently wanted goals. When everything feels like an emergency, it is hard to be gentle with ourselves.

Measure effort, not results. Keep track of efforts, not results, when you need to measure your progress. Results are outside our control most of the time. Set kind, achievable metrics, starting where you are. "This is what I can do today." At times, you will do the work of finding frozen places inside, listening to their stories, and allowing them closer to the present.

At times, simply staying alive is an overwhelming effort. Still here the next morning? Good, you are doing everything you can do.

At times, we are navigating uncertain terrain through a transition. It takes effort to sit with uncertainty and listen for internal and external signals about what comes next.

At times, we are exhausted. Unrelenting effort has not resolved the current difficulties. Give yourself permission to rest, even though nothing is resolved. Sometimes taking the pressure off is exactly what needs to happen, especially if the problem is not in us at all, but in our environment and the people around us.

We are not to blame for our pain. Sometimes we have to stop digging at a wound to let it heal. We might be internally repeating self-hating behavior learned from abusive treatment as a child. Taking a break can help interrupt those patterns.

Listen to internal warnings. It is useful to learn to manage and work with triggers, and it is also useful to get away from situations that continue to trigger distress. Not all distress is from the past. When our finely tuned warning systems tell us something is wrong, we can accept that as valid and turn toward ourselves to listen. The more we make room for our truth, the more we can connect with the present.

Past vs. present. We can find a middle way between discounting all hypervigilance and anxiety as PTSD symptoms, and believing that all our responses are only about the present. Everyone's reactions are influenced strongly by the past, with or without trauma.

We might believe that healing includes a way to tell immediately whether an internal response applies to the past or the present. Instead, healing gives us more tools to handle our responses, and more practice discerning patterns.

Some responses out of the past might become familiar, old friends back for a visit. Some responses to present-time manipulation or boundary violations might also become familiar, clear warning signals. Some responses might be hard to untangle no matter how much experience we have, confusing mixes of past and present.

Incorporated, not erased. Healing does not have an

endpoint, a time when everything is smoothed over perfectly as if the trauma never happened. Healed trauma is incorporated, not erased.

In my practice, clients often come in expecting to work hard and experience painful emotions. Sometimes, what the body needs is a relaxing massage. Experiencing rest and safety in the present is deeply healing.

How do you want to feel? Imagine how you want to feel when you are healed, or how someone else healed from trauma would feel. Make choices that help you feel that way. Someday, you will look around and notice that you feel that way a lot of the time. If traumatic material comes up, you will have the skills and experience to quickly return to balance. Taking breaks and moving slowly are intrinsic parts of the process.

When I Started

When I started healing* from abuse, I was a grad student. After many years in school, I knew all about graduation requirements, prerequisites, and homework assignments. I tackled the project with youthful enthusiasm. Surely, as soon as I could do all the right things and get them checked off by the right people, I would graduate into a sunny, welcoming world of healed, "normal" people. If I thought about time frames at all, I imagined it would take around 1-5 years, like a graduate degree.

I learned that it was my fault my relationships fractured, because I had never learned about boundaries and clear communication. I studied! I practiced! I agonized over my failures! Finally I learned that it had never been my fault, or at least, not only my fault. Once I had clear boundaries and clear communication, people got angry with me because they could no longer manipulate me easily, and that has become the reason I lack strong relationships.

I adopted the Serenity Prayer: "Grant me serenity to accept the things I cannot change; courage to change the things I can; and wisdom to know the difference." It took a painfully long time to realize and accept that I could not change other people, no matter how hard I worked to change myself to influence them. It took even longer to realize that I

---

* This essay was written for the anthology *We Have Come Far: Shared wisdom from survivors of extreme trauma* edited by Ani Rose Whaleswan, Sojourn Press, 2014.

mostly could not change myself, either. I could only begin to change how I treat myself. It takes courage to move from self-contempt to self-compassion.

I wish someone had told me from the beginning that I did not need fixing. I was fine just as I was right then, that minute. There was no way to fix myself enough to please the people trying to control me. I wish someone had told me from the beginning that body weight was not something I needed to fix or control. I recognize my need for those messages by the sense of relief and renewed possibility I feel when I encounter them.

I wish someone had told me over and over that the abuse was not my fault. Not the overt abuse, nor the subtle gaslighting, nor the abandonment either. None of it was my fault. It took years to name my PTSD, shame, and anxiety. A lot of healing has been about naming what happened, naming my responses, and most of all naming other people's responsibility for their actions.

I learned that there is no unwinding back to babyhood and rewinding with the nourishing childhood I should have had. Time has passed. In middle age I carry neediness awkwardly, on my own.

My health has deteriorated despite my best efforts at self-care. My social networks have frayed and dispersed despite my best efforts at communication and kindness. I still seek for a future where I feel calm and whole, but it seems I missed the turnoff despite all my watching for it. Nobody taught me how to deal with failure or defeat in a healthy way. No one told me it is part of life sometimes not to get what I most want, no matter how hard I work to get it.

I learned that rather than being a tiny exception, abuse is woven throughout society in racism, sexism, homophobia, ableism, and all the other ways society is tipped to favor one group over another. I learned that many people deal with many kinds of defeat every day. "There is an abuse-free way to get my needs met," sometimes helps me find creative solutions, and sometimes is simply not true.

I learned to patch together bits and pieces of support, and to grit my teeth through the times when the patchwork disintegrates. I learned to listen to my inner guidance about whom to trust and whom to avoid. Even when it changes. Even when it seems wrong. My relationship with myself is the one constant in a shifting world. I am grateful to the kernel of determination to survive that keeps me searching for the next bit of support.

In times of desperation, I can sometimes remember the mantra, "I give thanks for help unknown already on the way." Comfort, support, and safety do come along, whispers in comparison with the shouts of trauma.

After years of thinking I could not possibly do it right, I am grateful I started meditating. During meditation, anything I do is right, even if it would not meet anyone else's standards. It provides a tiny starting point of safety and calm. When, after all this time, I drop into a body memory or flashback, meditation practice helps me name it, and breathe, and know I will get through it.

I did not come out of grad school with the degree I initially sought, and my healing process did not neatly terminate in the warm, cozy life I aimed for. In the last twenty-three years, I have learned that healing is about undoing rather than doing, unlearning rather than learning. Unlearning the habit of looking to others for direction and validation. Unlearning the pervasive terror. Unlearning the leap out of my body.

Healing is not about getting somewhere else, but about fully being where I am, physically and emotionally, with all the flaws I thought I could erase someday. Healing is ongoing. I grieve for what I thought I could accomplish, and feel hesitant pride in what I have accomplished. It seems a small showing, but it is hard-won, and mine.

It has been a gift to know other survivors, and to help some of them heal. I stand with fellow victims and survivors and tell you that you do not need fixing. When you face defeat, I can tell you life is like that sometimes and none of it is your fault.

The Heartbreak of "Why?"

The question of "Why?" weaves over and under and through all the other reactions to trauma. Why did that happen? Why did it happen to me? Why didn't anyone help? Why couldn't I change it?

"Why?" engages our spiritual beliefs about the world and our own worth. If we believe in a Higher Power, we wrestle with why that power allows harm to continue. If not, we wrestle with why harm happens at random.

"Why?" can also be specific and personal. Why didn't my mother see I needed help? Why did my neighbor intentionally hurt me? Why didn't I avoid the car crash? While these questions could carry neutral curiosity, they are usually agonizingly judgmental.

Explaining with self-blame. "Why?" can be an urgent matter of survival, especially for children enduring abuse. We need to make sense of our world to continue functioning, and we often come up with an explanation that makes other people's cruel behavior all our fault. We accuse ourselves of "being too needy" or "wanting love" or "being seduced (or seductive)" or "should have known better" or "needed to learn a lesson."

Lesson: it's not your fault. When we experience trauma, we ask "What's the lesson here?" as if everything is planned in advance like a school curriculum, as if some people are in supporting roles for other people's story lines, as if we could avoid pain by being good enough. I believe we are each the star of our own story, and our stories interact in unpredictable ways.

Some people find comfort in the idea that we choose our parents before birth. I cannot believe that any soul or higher power would be so cruel as to choose some of the abusive and neglectful parenting out there. Everyone deserves and expects attuned, loving parents.

We can choose to learn from everything that happens to us even though the lesson is not planned in advance. Sometimes, the lesson is that it is not our fault and we cannot afford to internalize other people's bad behavior. Blame is like a hot potato being passed around, and we can simply refuse to accept it.

Sense of brokenness. Each of us is valuable simply because we exist, our unique selves worthy of cherishing and protection. When we blame ourselves for abuse, a core sense of our intrinsic value gets overlaid with a painful certainty of brokenness, badness, and deserving harm.

That certainty gets locked into an untouchable kernel, radioactive with shame. We flinch away from it defensively, and yet each loss or failure brings us back to the heartbreak of believing we are broken.

Gentle contact. When we set out to welcome and eventually integrate that isolated part, we might find another part that strongly rejects the kernel of self-blame. "I want nothing to do with you." Both parts are doing their best to protect us and survive. We can make gentle contact to say hello and let them know we hear them. The contact can be as brief as we need it to be. This process requires as much permission to be exactly where we are as we can scrape together.

In some ways, the rejecting part is right. It is not true that the abuse is our fault. No one deserves abuse for any reason.

The shame we carry belongs to the perpetrators, and to the people who failed to protect us. When we acknowledge the shame, we can also drop it, return it to the earth for recycling.

Shame vs. guilt. In her TED talk "Listening to Shame"*, Brene Brown defines guilt as, "I made a mistake," and shame as "I am a mistake." We all make mistakes, large and small. We choose our behavior, and we can choose to change it. No matter what we believe we did wrong, we can learn new patterns. We are not doomed to continue being hurt because of some inherent flaw.

Different questions. We can ask a different set of questions. Why did I survive? Why do I search for healing? What helped me from inside? What helped me from outside?

Maybe humans came through and helped in all the right ways. Maybe humans completely fell down on the job, and that seems normal because that is how it was. What non-human help came through? It might be a pet, or Spirit, or Nature, or music, or books.

Abuse is visible. To children being abused, it seems that the world is determinedly oblivious to their pain. It is an easy leap to assume that their pain does not matter, and they do not matter, to anyone.

From an adult's side, it looks different. An adult may suspect or even be certain that a child is being abused, but not be in a position to intervene. Calling Child Protective Services is a gamble, since they might not improve the situation. If we see an adult hurting a child in a grocery store, sometimes all we can do is give the child an acknowledging, loving look and move on. Even as adults we are afraid

---

* Brene Brown, "Listening to Shame"
ted.com/talks/brene_brown_listening_to_shame

of abusers, and our cultural narrative is that other people's struggles are none of our business.

Infrastructure for intervention. In a better world, we would have cultural narratives for how to intervene in abusive situations. There would be immediately accessible safe places for children and adults who are being hurt. There would be mandatory, compassionate, effective education for abusers to learn how to treat people with respect. We would all know that abuse is the fault of the perpetrator, and we would stop rewarding abusive and controlling behavior as a society.

It's not you. The heartbreak we feel in response to the sense of being broken tells us that underneath we remember wholeness. No matter how much we surrender to feeling at fault, we have a light inside that knows better.

I have a longtime dear friend who consistently tells me, "It's not you," when I share yet another interpersonal tangle. I finally posted a note repeating that several times to remind myself of his kind wisdom. Other people's cruelty is not our fault. What note can you post for yourself to ease the heartbreak of "Why"?

When we sit with "Why?" from a place of neutral curiosity rather than self-blame, some answers might float up about other people's stories. Maybe she was too afraid to confront him. Maybe he was too dissociated from his own child-self to treat a child with care. We each have to make our difficult peace with the question of "Why do people behave in evil ways?"

Worthy of Protection

Trauma survivors often struggle to accept needing care and protection from others.

When my friends entrust their two-month-old daughter to my arms, I feel instinctively, physically protective. My body wants to curl around her to keep her safe and well.

I feel emotionally protective of people I mentor, wanting to metaphorically spread my arms wide and shield them from politics and ill-will. Feeling protective of them does not diminish my recognition of their competence, strength, and ability to take care of themselves.

A baby's first job is to elicit protection and nurturing from a mother figure in order to survive. Growing children need to feel cherished both for their vulnerability and for their developing competence.

Not guard nor rescuer. Protection is not an armed guard at the door, active only when there is a threat. Protection is not a Rescuer looking down on a Victim and fearing a Perpetrator in a Drama Triangle.

Loving watchfulness. Protection is ongoing loving watchfulness, keeping the child's well-being in mind. Protection is gentle hands and a kind voice. Protection is not only respecting the child's boundaries, but teaching them to recognize and express their boundaries.

Protection draws a wider boundary, creating a home base where the child can relax and sense safety, where they know they belong. From there, the child can explore and take risks, knowing that someone has their back, and they can return to home base whenever they want. Protection is part of secure attachment.

Healthy entitlement. A protected child feels a healthy entitlement to have their needs heard and met. They know their wants are important because they experience attuned attention to what makes them happy. They internalize the sense of protection as well as the right to be protected.

Missing protection. A child who is protected only for being fragile, without recognition of the ways they are strong, learns that they have to choose between protection and strength. They miss the support of being valued for all of themselves.

A child who is neglected or abused feels the lack of protection as a sign of their own lack of value. Instead of asking what is wrong with their parents for not caring, they ask what is wrong with them. Their Inner Critic tries to change them to deserve protection. Their Inner Nurturer argues that they always already deserved protection.

An unprotected child experiences the world without a bubble of safety around them. Their parents may guard them from some threats, and even restrict them "for their safety" in a controlling way, but guarding only increases the sense of threat instead of generating a sense of safety.

Walking into danger. An unprotected child might not seek out protection or recognize when it is offered, because it is outside their experience. At the same time, they may feel intense shame about neediness, vulnerability, and longing for protection.

When I came home from middle school one day and walked in on some men robbing the house, it did not occur to me to run to the kind neighbors across the street for help.

When the robbers left me with my hands tied, it did not occur to me to dial 911, even though, as a white girl, I could expect them to help me. As I struggled to dial a friend's number on the old-fashioned rotary phone, it did not occur to me that the operator who spoke on the line was offering help. I froze and waited until she went away before returning to my struggle.

I did finally connect with my friend, who called the police, who came and untied me. Despite fingerprint powder scattered everywhere, they did not catch anyone. It is only now, looking back, that I see some of the options I had then.

Sense into protection. When you think about protection, what do you sense inside? Was it a comfortable background growing up, something you could take for granted? Do you have people around you now who care about your wellbeing? How do you respond when you encounter someone who clearly does not care?

Or do you feel a void, confusion about how protection might feel? Do you push down a desire for protection, afraid of revealing vulnerability or need? Protection might feel like basking in warm sunlight after a long cold winter, or like finding shelter from a rainstorm.

Inherited lack of protection. By default, lack of protection moves down generations and across society. People learn to hate their own vulnerability, and react negatively to others who dare to be vulnerable, whether as babies, children, or adults. We shame each other and ourselves for neediness, rather than simply acknowledge it.

Invite protection. We can break that cycle, and quiet some of the internal yelling and criticism, when we let our own protectiveness meet our neediness inside.

Imagine holding a baby or pet, or stopping traffic for a

child to cross, or watching someone succeed at something you taught them. How does protectiveness feel in your experience, in your body? Sense for an anchor for this feeling, a way to return to it.

Invite neediness. Now open a space inside for neediness to arise. It can be a small space, carefully contained, or a larger space with softer boundaries. Allow the neediness to be there, and acknowledge its presence. Is there something in you that feels the need to fix or suppress it? Acknowledge that, too. How do neediness and vulnerability feel in your experience, in your body?

Gently move back and forth between protectiveness and neediness, spending some time in each place. Can they both be present at the same time? Do they remain the same, or do they change in each other's presence? Say hello to whatever you notice.

Needs are a sign of health. As humans, as mammals, we are hard-wired to need touch, warmth, support, connection, love. Those needs will spring up no matter how much we were hurt, and no matter how hard we try to eradicate them. We can give those longings a little more room inside, a little more acknowledgment that they are a sign of health, not brokenness. We all deserve protection for our needy, vulnerable places as well as recognition of our strengths.

Integration: Live into Both/And

Live the questions now. Perhaps you will then gradually, without noticing it, live along some distant day into the answer. — Rainer Maria Rilke

Integration, healing, wholeness, unity. Many people equate the removal of divisions with the attainment of spiritual enlightenment. Integration can also mean acceptance, coordination, working well together, as when we integrate someone into a team. Integration is held out as the holy grail of trauma healing, both integrating trauma memories into narrative memory, and integrating younger parts into a fully functional adult.

Integration can be invited, but not forced. It happens along the way as part of healing, but cannot be rushed. It is a surrender to the truth of our experiences.

Separation as a circuit breaker. Parts fracture away to contain experiences, emotions, or impulses that are unmanageably overwhelming, like a circuit breaker interrupting a circuit to keep the wires from melting. None of those parts are disposable or unimportant, even if we sometimes want to discard the experiences they hold.

Sveta's Septembers. Every September, Sveta gets anxious and depressed. She thinks of those 30 days as a terrifying gauntlet she has to run every year, gritting her teeth through each moment and relaxing with relief on the first of October. She knows not everyone experiences September that way, but it feels like an inescapable fact of being herself, like her physical height.

Her Septembers are a combination of flashback and emergency mode, a set of seasonal triggers that bring up frozen-in-time memories of abuse at school long ago. As long as the part holding those memories is only around at that time of year, and she is hunkered down in survival mode, her Septembers will continue unchanged.

The separation of responsibilities allowed Sveta to survive the abuse. One part knows only abuse, only terror and hunkering down. Other parts kept going to class and doing homework and answering, "Fine!" when people asked how she's doing.

Pushing pain away. When a part causes us pain or embarrassment, our first thought is to push it away as much as possible. Those pesky child parts with their ungovernable emotions and behaviors remind us that the abuse really happened.

It is uncomfortable to think and talk about abuse. People reflexively defend the abuser ("I took a class from him, and I never had a problem!"), criticize us ("Why didn't you tell anyone at the time?"), or treat us like damaged goods.

We come out of dissociation the way we went in. How we respond to the prospect of integration is part of the process itself. Self-hatred might bubble up, or fury, or a belief that nothing and no one will ever help. We push the idea of integration away just as we originally pushed the trauma away, until one day something shifts.

Agreeing to get closer. Many people hope that integration will erase trauma and make them "normal". In contrast, true integration is inclusive, not exclusive. Nothing is lost, erased, or made less important, which might reassure child parts fighting against an adult part's agenda.

Integrating a part requires willingness to know and feel everything the part knows and feels. We might know a part's story, but knowing that something happened is like standing on shore contemplating a swim in a mountain lake. Integration is immersion in icy water.

Sveta begins the process of integration when she approaches her experience with genuine curiosity and acceptance. "I wonder why I get so scared in September," and, "It gets to be that way for as long as that's so." Another way to invite integration is to say out loud, "I'm willing to know what this is about."

Costs. Trauma and abuse are terrifying, enraging, miserable experiences. We push them away for good reason. When we agree to allow them closer, we experience physical and emotional echoes.

For Sveta, agreeing to let her younger part nearer means no sharp dividing line of relief on October first. It means not just knowing that she was abused, but feeling it happen, feeling nausea, pain, the smallness of her body then. "This happened to *me*." At the same time, she is aware of her present size and safety. Disturbing images overlay everyday life. She feels old terror and shame, framed by present awareness that all she has to do is breathe and let the feelings pass through her.

The deep processing of integration might make her spacy, distracted, tired, and irritable. She might want a lot of quiet time alone, or more time with kind friends than usual.

During integration, make space for raggedness, reduced functioning, having a hard time. Bring in as much nurturing support as you can. Allow yourself to mourn for any support you lack now, as well as back then. Allow yourself to celebrate the differences between present and past.

Benefits. After a while, integration is also coming out of that icy lake, drying off, and relaxing in the sun. The integrated part gets to experience present safety in addition to sharing difficult past memories. The shift might be sudden ("Wait, it wasn't my fault!") or gradual. The painful part of the process does come to an end.

Integration can lead to the unexpected revival of old interests and skills, like painting, or hiking, depending on what the fractured part carried away.

The divisions between parts are maintained with physical tension, blocking out awareness of different parts of the body. With integration, long held tension can release, leading to more comfort and ease of motion.

Completed integration can feel like putting down a weight, both emotionally and physically. The energy caught up in a wall between parts is available for daily life. Triggered reactions feel less overwhelming and happen less often.

Both/And. It makes sense to wish the abuse never happened, and to want to be someone it never happened to. At the same time, there is deep healing when we invite a younger part closer and say, "You matter. Your experience matters. Your truth matters. I accept you."

Sveta's October of integration was hard, but each September after that was easier. The abuse at school became one of many past stories that weave together into who she is today.

Resources

Ann Weiser Cornell's *The Radical Acceptance of Everything: Living a Focusing Life*, Calluna Press, 2005, contains articles with concrete examples of practical acceptance.

Radical Acceptance: Embracing Your Life with the Heart of a Buddha, Penguin Random House, 2004, by Tara Brach directly addresses how to be with feelings of "not good enough."

Debbie Ford's *The Dark Side of the Light Chasers: Reclaiming Your Power, Creativity, Brilliance, and Dreams*, Riverhead Books, 2010, contains detailed information and exercises about projection. In her examples, owning a projection magically changes the situation every time, which has not been my experience.

We Have Come Far: Shared wisdom from survivors of extreme trauma, Sojourn Press, 2014, edited by Ani Rose Whaleswan contains essays and poetry by 21 authors writing about their experiences after many years of healing.

Brene Brown has written several books on the topic of shame. *Daring Greatly: How the Courage to Be Vulnerable Transforms the Way We Live, Love, Parent, and Lead*, Avery Publishing Group, 2015, summarizes some of the previous ones.

In *The Emotionally Absent Mother: A Guide to Self-Healing and Getting the Love You Missed*, Experiment, 2010, Jasmin Lee Cori talks about many aspects of a Good Mother, including protector, home base, and place to rest.

Presence After Trauma

3: Body

Body acceptance can be especially challenging after trauma. Instead of "being" a body, we withdraw from our trauma-disrupted systems and "have" a body, reluctantly.

The physical body becomes both a threat and a resource. We might want to "just forget and move on," but the body remembers trauma concretely, inarguably, in full sensory and emotional detail. We might believe that the body failed back then for wanting and responding, or for fighting back ineffectually, or even for living through the trauma. Body-hatred might come from looking different from the current culturally "ideal" body, and from the effects of trauma in the present.

At the same time, the body remembers exactly who we are, concretely, inarguably. We may have had to compromise and surrender to survive, but the body remembers how we really feel, what we really want. The body bears the imprint of the past, but lives only in the present.

You can become more present in your body by learning about your structure and slowly reestablishing contact. Bodies are surprisingly accepting after abandonment. They do not sulk like a cat, but are simply relieved that you returned. "That's better."

You are the specific presence your body wants. You do not have to improve before deserving to be present in your body, just as your body does not have to improve to deserve your presence. You already belong together. Reconnecting with your body can restore a sense of belonging that seemed lost forever.

We become present into our bodies, with our bodies. Eventually we realize or acknowledge that we are our bodies. As we become more familiar with our structure, we can move more easily, possibly with less pain, and release barriers that hold back memories and emotions.

Humans Allowed Full Body

Oregon law allows bicyclists to use a full travel lane while turning left, passing another cyclist, or avoiding hazards such as glass, debris, and suddenly opened car doors. Stickers and signs announce, "Bicyclists Allowed Full Lane," because many drivers are unaware of the law and behave rudely when they are impatient to pass.

Humans are allowed full use of our bodies all the time. Many of us, especially women, are encouraged to make ourselves small, take up less space, and make sure we do not inconvenience those around us. Others of us, especially men, are encouraged to take up extra space without noticing how it affects those around us.

We own our interior space out to our edges, front to back, side to side, and crown of the head to soles of the feet. Take some time to sense your edges and interior space. In a slow sweep from feet to head, can you feel your clothing or the air against your skin all over, or are there places where you are numb or absent? Can you sense the quality of your skeleton's support?

Sense out to your edges in different environments over the next few days, or imagine yourself in different environments now. When do you tend to curl in protectively, and when do you allow yourself to relax? How much space do you own at home, as a guest, at work, on transit, in a car, on a bicycle? Do you ride your bike in the middle of a travel lane when you need to?

How much interior space do you own when you are standing near someone you know? How about next to a stranger? How does your relative level of privilege in society affect how you take up space near someone else? For example, imagine standing near a taller white man in a suit. Now imagine standing near a smaller Laotian woman in jeans. We subconsciously calculate how much space we deserve relative to others, responding to subtle signals of entitlement or deference.

Confidently occupy any size body. Fat-shaming is another way we are told to take up less space. The stigma around being large has little to do with health, since it has been repeatedly scientifically shown that "overweight" people live longer than those who are erroneously called "ideal weight" according to BMI charts.*

It has also been repeatedly scientifically shown that intentional weight-loss diets rarely results in sustained weight loss, and often result in overall weight gain in the long run. Our size is determined by complex factors, most of them outside our control. We deserve to confidently occupy any size body all the way out to the edges.

Trauma interrupts body awareness. Trauma almost always interrupts our ability to own our interior space. Sexual assault, physical assault, and even emotional abuse all give us the signal that others own our bodies. Taking back our bodies is a big part of the healing process.

When part of us gets frozen at a young age because of trauma, the sense of our body size is also frozen. Our internal bodymap may say our shoulders are only as wide as a

---

* Time Magazine - Being Overweight Is Linked to Lower Risk of Mortality. healthland.time.com/2013/01/02/being-overweight-is-linked-to-lower-risk-of-mortality/

four year old's even though we have grown to adult size. We can gently bring our perceptions up to date by sensing the details of our current size.

Our internal bodymap stops updating because we withdraw our awareness from that part of the body. The sensory memories stored there were too overwhelming back then, so they were sealed away. As we send exploratory awareness into that part, we may need to integrate the emotions and memories of that younger self along the way. Make room for that process to take all the time it needs.

Full-width shoulders. Sense the width of your shoulders, all the way to the outside of both upper arms. You can lean against a wall near a doorway or corner, and touch the wall at your outside shoulder. Leaving your hand in place, turn around to see your full width. Or, ask a friend to draw around you on a large piece of paper.

Your shoulder blades are toward the outside of that width. Put a hand over the top of the opposite shoulder where your arm connects. Curve your arm forward and then back and feel your shoulder blade move. The shoulder blades may be further from your spine than you expect. Your arms are suspended from an extension of the shoulder blades to give them space from the ribs.

Deep, wide, short lungs. Now move your hand down to the side of your torso, under your armpit. Breathe in, and feel your ribs swing up and your torso widen and deepen as your lungs expand. Let the breath flow out, and feel the ribs settle back to their resting positions.

Your lungs start above your collarbones and descend to the top of the diaphragm's dome, right at your bra's band if you wear one, at around the seventh rib on the out breath. At no time does air enter your belly, although the intestines do push outward as the diaphragm descends to pull air into the lungs.

Your lungs are deep, wrapping around the spine in back, and wide, filling the torso, nestled around the heart. Breathe in, allowing all that space to fill with air, and then allow it to empty again.

Place your hands gently on the opposite upper arms and sense for movement in your shoulders and arms as you breathe in and out. If they are not braced, they move with the ribs they rest on.

Full-width hips. Now rest your hands on the widest part of your hips. Keeping them at the same width, move your hands out in front of you. Is their distance surprising? Your hips may be narrower or wider than you expect, and you might have absorbed cultural judgments about what size they "should" be. How does it feel to give them permission to be exactly as wide as they are?

Full-body movement. Imagine a stressful environment, where you walk or roll while taking up as little space as possible. Shoulders and hips are narrow, breathing is constrained.

Now, imagine an environment where you can walk or roll comfortably and confidently, allowing your arms to swing from the full width of your shoulders. Your lungs have a lot of room to expand in your wide and deep torso. Similarly, your legs swing at the sides of the full width of your pelvis, without restriction.

Which type of environment is more familiar? Which takes more energy? Notice who, if anyone, is present in the two scenes, and what else differs between them.

Full-body emotions. When we make ourselves small, we restrain our emotions. When we are connected with all of ourselves, we make room for our emotions to move freely through us, each one cresting and then ebbing away in its turn. Emotions usually feel less overwhelming when they have more space to spread out.

As children, many of us were told not to be so loud, and not to have such extravagant emotions. "I'll give you something to cry about." "What gives you the right to be so happy?" "Something will pop your bubble soon enough." As adults, our emotions are allowed to take up space. We do not need someone else's permission or group consensus to be sad enough to cry, angry enough to stomp around, or happy enough to dance.

Claim yourself. Trauma and society push us to stay numb and endure. Our inner aliveness pushes us to expand, feel, breathe, play. Our bodies move more smoothly and easily with full awareness. Claim your inner terrain for yourself. It is your birthright.

Explore Uncurled Posture

When we feel threatened, we hunch protectively around our center. Neck scrunches, shoulders pull in, belly tightens, legs press together. When the threat passes, we relax into a more comfortable posture. If the threat remains active for a long time, or if we stay in emergency mode after trauma, our muscles remain protectively tense, even when we try to relax.

Years of tension lead to pain, and we withdraw our awareness from the tense areas. We fight the tension as if it were external to us, stretching fiercely or asking others to dig in and relax our muscles for us. We criticize our own posture and obey injunctions to "stand up straight!" by pulling against existing tension, adding even more tension.

Begin exploring. During this exploration, say hello to what you sense, and to whatever judgments arise in response. The goal is to perceive, connect, and make space for change, without expecting any particular result.

As you sit or stand or lie down, allow yourself to settle into your position. Sense into your relationship with the surface supporting you. Give yourself a long time to be exactly as you are: your usual, everyday self with your usual, everyday tension.

Check inside for movement. After a long time of resting into your usual position, follow an intake of breath into awareness of tension. Do you sense a pull, holding, tightness, or clenching that might want to lighten or let go from the inside? Is there any motion your body wants to make to get more comfortable? The sensation might be, "Oh, I didn't realize I was holding there!" as a shoulder drops, or "I have more room than I thought," as a hip moves back.

If you feel numb, you could invite awareness into tension by curling up more tightly than usual. Hold, hold, hold, then let go. Does anything feel different?

If some tension releases that was pulling against deeper tension, you might find yourself curling inward more. Allow this to happen. You might also find an impulse to uncurl from the inside, bringing your body into a more open posture. Rest into your new position for a while, then repeat the process.

Shifts happen. After a shift, you might notice a deeper breath, maybe with a catch in it, stomach rumbling, or a sensation of warmth. There might be a click or pop as bones readjust. Pain might ease, or sharpen briefly, or pulse and ache.

Belly tension. Follow a breath in, and let your attention settle down toward your belly. Is your belly soft, open, resilient, and receptive to the motion of your breath? Or is it held tightly, resisting the breath as it comes in and goes out?

You could bring a hand to meet your belly with gentle contact, sensing how that feels in both your belly and your hand.

Rest into your present experience with your belly and your breath. As your belly relaxes over time, you might find that your voice, your truth, and your emotions flow more freely.

The psoas muscles deep in the core (see figure, next page) often contribute to curled posture. They originate at the front of the lumbar spine on each side, interweaving at the top with the breathing diaphragm. From there they spill down over the front of the pelvis and wrap around the top of the femurs.

The main muscular action of the psoas is to flex the hip, bringing a leg closer to the belly. It also contributes to side-bending, sit-ups, and leg rotation at the hip.

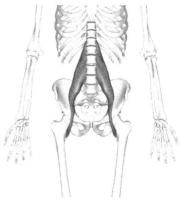

Psoas Muscles

Constructive rest. In her book *Core Awareness*, Liz Koch suggests many explorations for becoming more aware of the psoas muscles. One is constructive rest position, lying face up with the knees bent and feet flat on the floor. Sense into your experience in the present, and give your body ample time to rest into gravity and support.

After resting, you can experiment with allowing one leg at a time to lengthen slowly along the floor until fully extended. Do other muscles try to help? Be curious about how the motion could be easier. Can the leg float down and back up? You could stay with just the part of the motion that is easy, even when that is a tiny shift in position.

Lie on a foam roller. You can lie face up on a foam roller, with your spine along the length of the roller. Sit at one end, then gradually roll your spine down. This position asks your chest to open and your shoulders to slide back and down. A short rest on the roller can disrupt a tension headache and show your body new posture options. A rolled up blanket or towel along the spine instead of the foam roller gives a more gentle stretch.

Uncurl your tail. When frightened, ashamed, or showing submission, animals tuck their tails between their legs. Humans have the same impulse, although our tailbones nestle inside the pelvis. When you put your hands on your hips with thumbs pointing back, then let your thumbs slide down and together along your sacrum, they point toward your tailbone.

Bring your awareness to that area from the inside, and invite your tail to uncurl. Allow the uncurling motion to propagate up your spine through each curve. At the top, your chin might tip down, allowing your gaze to take in more of the room. You might find that your belly softens, your shoulders drop, and your weight settles more firmly into your seat. Try uncurling your tail while standing and in motion as well.

Stand on the outsides of your feet. Curled posture includes pulling the legs together protectively, especially after sexual assault. This shifts the body's weight toward the inside of the feet. While standing, experiment with shifting your weight toward the outside edges of your feet. Sense into the springy lateral arch. This shift can allow your whole body to widen and give the sacrum more space at the SI joints, relieving chronic sacral or low back pain.

Surface awareness. Listening to tension often leads to awareness deeper in your body. Body mapping teacher Susan Riggs suggests also checking in with your surface, your skin. What do you sense about your contact with your clothing? With the air? You might find it easy to sense into some areas, while other areas might be numb or blank.

Explore anytime. You can do these explorations while sitting or standing still, or in bed at night. You can do them while walking, biking, or driving. You can weave them into a meditation practice. At first, little may happen, or the same place might release every time. Over time, the body can choose how tightly to curl and when to uncurl.

Let Your Jaw Speak

When the body curls protectively, the jaw often tightens as well.

Your **avenue of expression** includes your jaw, tongue, throat, and the surrounding muscles and bones that support you in making sound to communicate your thoughts and emotions. Physical movement in your avenue of expression creates sound. Immobility is silent.

Essential gateway. The mouth is a gateway to breath, nourishment, verbal expression, sensing taste and texture, and connecting to others through kissing and oral touch. Infants and young children enthusiastically explore their world by putting everything in their mouths. They freely express their emotions through crying, babbling, and eventually, words and song.

Healthy limits. As children grow, most encounter healthy limits on their exploration and expression. They learn about boundaries:

- When to use an "inside voice"
- When to explore with eyes and fingers instead of lips and tongue
- When to choose words to honor privacy and kindness
- To check with the recipient before bestowing affectionate kisses
- To listen to their bodies about what and when to eat

- To manage emotions internally in addition to letting them spill into sound

Healthy limits leave the avenue of expression lively, open and available.

Unhealthy limits. Too many children also encounter unhealthy limits in the form of punishment and shaming for their choices and expressions, silencing them. Family secrets, including abuse, are kept inside at all costs. Abuse may affect the mouth directly through forced feeding, blows, or oral rape. The whole body restrains the avenue of expression out of shame and fear. Jaw muscles become tight and resistant to relaxation.

Ongoing anger can also tighten jaw muscles. Double binds and oppression lead to swallowing anger rather than expressing it.

Gentle exploration. Check in with your jaw. Are your upper and lower teeth touching? Dentists remind us that our teeth only need to touch when chewing or swallowing. A clenched jaw can result in chronic TMJ (temporomandibular joint), neck, and head pain, as well as damaged teeth. A sling of muscles comfortably supports the jaw in a slightly open position.

Gently open and close your mouth a few times. Notice what happens in the rest of your body. Do you continue to breathe easily, or do you hold your breath? Do your neck and throat relax into the motion, or tighten? Are your shoulders resting down and back, or are they "helping" to move your jaw? Welcome anything you notice, including any judgments that pop up.

Movement from the inside. Your jaw is an open V shape that angles up at both ends to connect to your skull. Your mouth floor is filled by tongue root, not bone.

With friendly curiosity, experiment with movement in your jaw. Let your fingers ride along lightly just in front of your ears on your TMJs (jaw joints). Your jaw drops and slides at these joints. Your upper teeth are fixed, part of your skull. If the movements are jerky or asymmetrical, try moving more slowly or for a shorter distance.

Drop your jaw a little to create space between upper and lower teeth. Gently protrude your jaw forward away from your ears, and retract it back toward your ears. Move it from side to side. Let your mouth drop open, and close it again, maintaining a gap between your upper and lower teeth.

If you clench your jaw or grind your teeth at night, a few gentle movements at bedtime can remind your jaw that it has more options.

Self massage. The temporalis and masseter muscles (see figure) pull the jaw closed. They often like massage. Rub from the bottom of your jaw up to your cheekbone near your ears on both

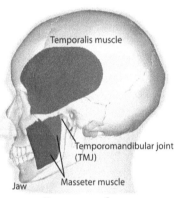

Jaw muscles

sides. The masseter is one of the strongest muscles in the body and might like a lot of pressure. Remember to touch with kindness as you experiment with deeper pressure.

To soothe the temporalis, rub up from your cheekbones and let your fingers fan out behind your eyes, above your ears, and along your temples. Move your fingers in different directions, and make little circles. Let your muscles tell you what feels good. Do you notice any difference in your jaw, head, or neck afterward?

Movement from the outside. Now put a friendly hand on the front of your jaw and wiggle it from side to side and up and down. Does your jaw allow the movement, or does it need to be in charge? What if your jaw and hand move together? The movement might be very small at first. Are other muscles, perhaps in your neck, shoulders, or belly, trying to help control your jaw? Open the door to relaxation with kind attention, rather than using force.

How does your jaw feel now? If it relaxed a little, you may notice yawns, deeper breaths, or borborygmus (belly rumbles). You may also notice emotions or thoughts associated with the tension. Do any judgmental voices arise? If you feel intensely negative about these experiments, those feelings might be stored in your jaw. Continue to extend kind attention to whatever you notice.

Safe space for expression. The avenue of expression becomes a battleground between authentic sound and silent self-protection. Our need to be heard struggles with our needs for approval and safety. As we listen to all our needs without taking sides or demanding change, we create safe space over time for relaxation, movement, and expression.

Sense Your Spine's Support

Support is an ongoing issue for trauma survivors. Lack of support makes an event more traumatic, and there is often inadequate support afterward as well. Trauma leads to dissociation, separating us from sensing internal and external physical support.

Many of us think of our spine as the knobs we feel running up the back of the torso, forgetting the sturdy column at our center. The back part of the spine protects the spinal cord which runs continuously from brain to sacrum, with nerves branching off at each vertebra. The central part of the spine is interleaved with supportive disks, providing responsive, flexible, weight-bearing support.

The spine is composed of 24 vertebrae plus the sacrum and tailbone. Four gentle curves provide springy resilience.

- 7 **cervical vertebrae** in the neck balance the heavy skull from its center.

- 12 **thoracic vertebrae** in the mid and upper back support 12 pairs of ribs in a beehive shape.

- 5 large **lumbar vertebrae** in the low back provide stable, central support for the whole torso.

- The **sacrum** is formed from 5 fused vertebrae. The sacrum transfers the torso's weight to

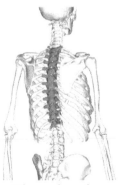

Thoracic spine highlighted

the pelvis and down to the legs. The **coccyx** (tail-bone) contains 3-5 small vertebrae and continues the sacral curve.

Solid support. Notice that the lumbar spine curves in to the center of the body. If you point your fingers in at the sides of your waist, you are pointing at your lumbar spine. Your body surrounds your spine, rather than being in front of it.

While seated, rock forward and back on your sit bones, and sense the movement of your lumbar spine. With small movements, push your lumbar spine toward the backrest, and then let it arch forward. Can you sense the flexible column of living bone within you? Say hello to it, and listen for any sensations, emotions, or images it shares with you.

One percent. When the body is in emergency mode, we expect support to loudly demand our attention. Settle into the surface under you, and allow one percent of the support into your body. Support might be easier to find when you listen for whispers rather than shouts.

Gather and lengthen. In addition to familiar bending and twisting motions, our spine gathers and lengthens, the vertebrae moving closer together and farther apart, with each breath and movement. The motion is intrinsic to your body, something to allow rather than make happen.

The lungs and heart nestle around the upper thoracic spine. As the surrounding ribs move up with each in-breath, the whole spine moves back and compresses slightly. As the ribs relax back down, the spine moves centrally and expands again. Lie face down over an exercise ball or pile of blankets and relax into a few big breaths to feel your spine gather and lengthen.

Lifted head. The cervical spine in your neck is aligned

vertically over the support of the lumbar spine. The topmost cervical vertebra, known as C1 or the atlas, cradles the skull and allows a slight nodding motion forward and back, as well as side to side. Can you feel your skull sliding gently on the atlas? When you curl your tongue inward, it points back along the roof of your mouth to where the base of your skull rests on the atlas. You can also point in just below your ear holes toward that central support.

The body is structured so our head can move freely wherever our attention directs. Tense muscles in our neck and shoulders pull our head down and back, interfering with effortless movement. Some of that tension may be left over from past startle reactions. Experiment with letting your jaw point down more than usual, drawing the back of your head up. Shoulders can relax when they are not responsible for the head's position.

Full movement. Gently explore the range of motion of your whole spine in all directions, bending forward and back, side-bending, and twisting. Are some movements more comfortable and familiar than others? Do you notice differences between your right and left sides?

Say hello to any pain you notice. Does it change as you continue to explore?

Allow your torso to move in relation to your legs, and your head to move in relation to your upper back. Do you feel more connected to some sections of your spine than others? Feel your continuous spine along the full length of your torso, from the bottom of your pelvis to your neck. Allow movement to ripple all the way from the base of your skull to the tip of your tailbone.

Swim through air. Next time you go for a walk, notice how your spine moves with your steps. Experiment with allowing motions to be larger. Can you allow your head to float on a lengthened spine? Let your movements originate from your spine, like a fish swimming through air.

Ease and comfort. After trauma, it can feel like everything is difficult. When we feel our bones reliably support our body and movement, we regain a long-lost sense of ease and comfort. As we remember how to trust our structure, our muscles can do less work and the whole body relaxes, expands, and breathes more easily.

Arms Relate to the World

Our arms reach out to connect to the world and bend in to defend us from threats. We pull in what we want and push away what we do not want, physically expressing our boundaries.

If our efforts to relate to the world are repeatedly thwarted, we unconsciously inhibit impulses, limit movement, and dissociate from our arms.

Preventing people from expressing boundaries renders them vulnerable to manipulation and control, and is a red flag for abuse. Do you reach out freely? Do you feel comfortable pushing away what you do not want? Women, people of color, and other marginalized groups are actively discouraged from expressing and enforcing boundaries.

Explore your structure. To reclaim your capacity to relate to the world freely, explore the structure of your shoulders, arms, and hands with kind attention and touch. Regaining awareness of these bones and joints can help resolve nagging pain and enlarge the available range of motion for your arms.

Take a moment to notice your shoulders and arms from the inside. Do they feel heavy or light? Do you feel the touch of clothing, air, or a surface they are resting on? What do you notice from the palms of your hands? The backs? Say hello to each joint with gentle movements.

Independent shoulder girdle. The shoulder girdle is structurally separate from the beehive-shaped rib cage, attached only at the sternum (breastbone). On each side, the clavicle (collarbone) sweeps past the first rib to meet the scapula (shoulder blade), which extends out from the back upper ribs to meet it. The shoulder girdle is centered over the pelvis, easily supported by the weight-bearing spine.

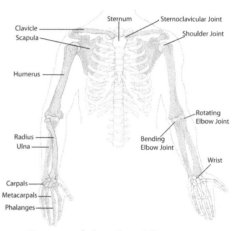

Bones of the shoulder, arm, and hand

Each scapula attaches to the ribs with flexible muscles, allowing them to move independently. The ribs can rise like bucket handles with the breath, and the scapulas can move up, down, and around the rib cage. Pull them back toward your spine, then down toward the floor, then curve them up and forward toward your ears. Move one at a time in a circle. If the movements are jerky or painful, try making them smaller and slower.

Bouncy castle around the heart. Our shoulders often take on extra jobs that prevent them from moving freely. They hunch protectively around our core, pull toward the spine in an effort to take up less space, or guard our neck to silence our avenue of expression. What patterns of tension or resistance do you notice when you invite your shoulders to move?

The heart is naturally protected in its own bouncy castle*

---

* Amy Bennett, LMT, personal communication, 2014

even when the shoulders relax down and back. The heart rests on the flexible dome of the diaphragm, surrounded by the lungs, moving with each breath. The thoracic spine and ribs provide supportive walls. Feel your heart beat as it dances with your breath. How do your shoulders want to relate to your heart?

Unfamiliar joint with a long name. Unlike the shoulder, elbow, and wrist, the first arm joint does not have a familiar name. The sternoclavicular joints are where each clavicle (collarbone) meets the sternum (breastbone).

Find one of your clavicles below your neck (see figure) and follow it toward the midline of your body until it ends at the sternum. Rest a gentle hand there as you move your shoulder on that side forward, back, and around. If you do not feel movement, try smaller motions. It may take time to convince your brain that movement is available there. Move each side separately, then both together.

Cooperative shoulder joint. The humerus (upper arm bone) forms the shoulder joint with an extension of the scapula out to the side, meeting at an area about the size of your thumb. Hold one scapula steady with the opposite hand over your shoulder to explore the humerus's range of motion. Notice how far you can move your arm up and reach forward with the scapula held still.

Release your scapula and allow it to move with the humerus as you reach up and forward. How far can you reach now? The scapula and humerus work together for large arm movements. Invite them to move smoothly together. Does anything get in the way of their cooperation?

Two elbow joints. Your forearm has two long bones, the ulna on the pinky finger side, and radius on the thumb side. The ulna forms the familiar bending elbow joint with the humerus. The radius rotates at the humerus, allowing the hand to turn. Rest a hand palm up, and feel the movement at your elbow when you turn your hand palm down. With your other hand, follow the radius as it crosses the ulna, as illustrated on the left side of the figure.

Wrists align pinkies with forearms. Below the knobs at the ends of the forearm bones, each wrist has eight small rounded bones in two arched rows. In its home position, the wrist aligns the pinky finger with the ulna in a straight line. Imagine picking up a suitcase or hanging from a bar and notice the alignment of your wrists. We create unnecessary strain when we align our thumb with the radius instead.

How do your arms and shoulders feel when you allow your pinky fingers to rest in a straight line with your forearms? Experiment with typing and other motions. You may notice a sense of spaciousness, overall relaxation, and reduced effort. Repetitive strain injuries (RSI) can heal when we move with less strain.

Manipulative hands. Our hands manipulate our environment, changing it to suit us. The thumb points out to the side and rotates at the wrist, allowing it to meet the other fingers. Each finger starts, not at the palmar crease, but below it. Gently hold a finger as it moves and feel the first finger joint opposite the knuckle.

Move comfortably. Let your arms rest at your sides with a new awareness of your structure. Notice how it feels to reach out, push away, and bend them protectively. Choose a new piece of information to experiment with as you move through your day.

The more we cooperate with our body's structure, the more comfortable we are in movement and at rest, and the more clearly we can physically express our boundaries.

Change the Rules, Inhabit Your Pelvis

There are many reasons to proceed slowly and with compassion as you consider connecting with your pelvis. The bony structure of your pelvis provides a neutral starting point for awareness.

Do you inhabit your pelvis, or is it a numb absence at your center? Curious toddlers and maturing adolescents absorb their parents' discomfort with the pelvic area. Sexual abuse survivors detour around painful memories stored there.

Cultural rules encourage us to withdraw awareness from our pelvis except during sex, and maybe even then. The pelvis is not only the site of sexuality, reproduction, and elimination. Awareness in your pelvis can help balance your whole body and allow you to move from your center.

Strong emotions. You may believe your hips are too wide, or too narrow. You may feel shame about sexual feelings. You may struggle with incontinence, constipation, infertility, or chronic pain.

Hands on hips. When you put your hands on your hips as if scolding someone, your hands rest on your iliac crests, the upper curve of your pelvic bones (see figures, next page). What sensations do you notice as you rest your hands there? You might notice pressure, tingling, warmth, irritation, blankness, or absence.

Living bone. Our bones, pink with nourishing blood, form living, responsive anchors in our bodies. Pressing gently, you can follow the curve forward to the front of your hips, and back to the base of your spine. Imagine living as that solid curve of bone. What qualities come to mind? To me, that curve feels strong, open, and capable.

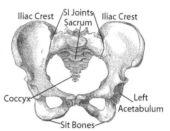

Wide, rounded pelvis

Support for the spine. The thick, triangular bone at the back of the pelvis is the sacrum. In standing or sitting, it transmits support from the pelvis to the spine, which emerges from the top of the triangle.

Rest a hand on your sacrum. It might be more comfortable to use the back of your hand. How does that feel from the inside? You might notice coolness,

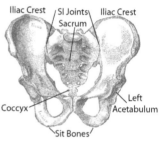

Narrow, angular pelvis

numbness, prickling, steadiness, or nothing. Imagine how it feels to be a sacrum. Do you notice any difference from your contact with your iliac crests?

Mobile joints. The angled surfaces on the sides of the sacrum where it meets each ilium form the sacroiliac (SI) joints. Although strong ligaments keep the bones close together, these are mobile joints. When muscles are tense, ligaments are strained, or bones are immobilized, the SI joints can be a source of low back pain.

Using both thumbs, find the back of your SI joints, on average farther apart for cis* female than cis male bodies.

---

* The cis prefix describes someone whose gender identity matches their anatomical gender. On average, cis female bodies tend toward wider pelvises with a rounder opening, adapted for childbearing. Any individual's pelvis shape is normal for them.

You can follow the iliac crests around, or follow your spine down, or ask your intuition to guide your hands. The SI joints might be sore when you press on them.

Tail bones. At the lower tip of the sacrum, we have the remnants of a tail, 3-5 tail bones forming the coccyx. They curve away from the surface of the body, but you might be able to feel the first one at the bottom of your sacrum. Can you bring awareness to your coccyx? These unassuming little bones can come to our attention suddenly if cracked in a fall, making sitting painful for months.

Bones in motion. Allow your weight to settle into your pelvis. If you sit on one hand and rock forward and back, you can feel your ischial tuberosity (sit bone) on that side, at the bottom of your pelvic structure. Like the SI joints, the sit bones are also on average farther apart for cis female than cis male bodies. Yours may be wider or narrower than you expect.

On each side, the rounded head of your femur (thigh bone, see figure, page 106) connects to the acetabulum, a hollow on the outside of your pelvis just above the sit bone. Slowly stand up. Can you feel the bones moving? Now that you are standing, can you feel your pelvis supporting your upper body? What happens if you give your pelvis permission to rest more deeply on your supporting legs? Bend forward at the hips to feel your pelvis rotating on your femurs.

Pelvic tilt. Standing upright, gently tilt your pelvis forward and back. What muscles help you make that movement? How does your spine respond to the change at its foundation? Do you notice any shifts in your feet? Do you have an emotional response to the different positions? Come back to your usual standing position and notice how you hold your pelvis.

In her beautifully researched and illustrated book *8 Steps to a Pain-Free Back*, Esther Gokhale recommends that we allow the top of the pelvis to tilt forward so that the sacrum is higher in the back. If we still had a tail, it would flow out behind us instead of being tucked between our legs.

The tucked pelvic position has only been considered good posture for about a hundred years in Europe and the United States. Other cultures have maintained a more structurally aligned good posture with a forward-tilted pelvis supporting a relatively straight back and rolled-back shoulders. How does it feel to allow the top of your pelvis to tilt forward?

Take up space. Now that you have explored the bony structure and motion of your pelvis, take a deep breath and allow the bones to settle comfortably. Where do they want to be in relation to each other? In relation to your feet? Your spine? Allow yourself all the space you need to find ease.

What works for you? As you move through your day, check in with your pelvis. What sensations do you notice as you sit, stand, and walk? When you inhabit your pelvis, you gain direct information about what works for you, rather than relying on external rules.

Legs Dance, Kick, Run

Our legs help us defend ourselves, move around, dance in celebration, and connect to the earth. They make up approximately thirty percent of our body mass, offering a large space to help us manage emotions.

Survival responses. Our whole body mobilizes in an emergency, including our legs. They might want to kick as part of a fight response or run as part of a flight response. They might want to stay closed to defend against rape. They might get "weak-kneed" and collapse as part of a freeze response when escape seems impossible.

The intense mobilization in the legs often gets suppressed rather than used. We disconnect from our legs, losing our connection to movement, grounding, and a reservoir for emotion.

We can reconnect by understanding our structure and sensing into our legs. When the suppressed energy starts to move again, you might notice trembling, heat, or tingling. In its wake, you might notice increased delight in the present moment.

Natural variation. Human legs vary in girth, length, proportion, strength, flexibility, smoothness, and hairiness. We quickly learn to judge our legs for how they appear to others rather than embrace them as an integral part of ourselves. Especially for women, "ideal" legs are attainable for a select few in adolescence and become increasingly unlikely as we age.

Legs also vary in their ability to bear weight, walk, run, sit comfortably, and move without pain. Despite the Americans with Disabilities Act (ADA) passed in 1990, our constructed environment is still unnecessarily difficult to navigate for people who use mobility aids such as wheelchairs, scooters, and baby strollers.

Relate to your legs. As you learn more about their structure, notice how you relate to your legs. You might find friendliness, judgment, numbness, distance, gratitude, anger, and other emotions and attitudes.

Also notice how your legs relate to you. When you listen to them, what do you hear? You might get sensory information, impulses toward movement, associations with the past, numbness, or emptiness. If you rarely reach out to your legs, you might notice resentment or loneliness at first. The body is usually quick to forgive and happy to reconnect.

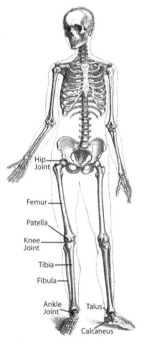

Hips at the sides. When we put "hands on hips", our hands actually rest on the iliac crests of the pelvis. The hip joints, where the femurs (thigh bones) meet the pelvis, are below the iliac crests on each side, about four inches down. The outside top of the femur has a knob you can feel when you push in gently. (See figure.)

Stick figures and dolls often incorrectly show legs sticking out of the bottom of a square torso, angling out

Bones of the leg, ankle, and foot

from the center, or hinging forward and back. In truth,

- Our legs are on our sides, like our arms, and start above the hip crease.
- The femurs are separated by the width of the pelvis and angle in toward the knees.
- Our legs rotate forward, back, and to the side with a ball-and-socket joint.

When we stand, our pelvis and legs make a strong arch to support us. When we sit, our legs rotate out of the way to allow our torso to rest on the rounded sit bones.

Broad knees. The knee is a hinge joint where the broad end of femur meets the supportive head of the tibia (larger bone of the lower leg). The patella (kneecap) floats in front of the femur, above the main joint. Bend and straighten your legs and feel the broad area of contact and movement in your knees.

The fibula, the smaller lower leg bone on the pinky toe side, meets the tibia below the knee.

Hidden ankles. The knobs that we often think of as our ankles are the ends of the tibia on the inner leg and fibula on the outer leg. The ankle joint is under and between the knobs, a hinge joint between the two lower leg bones and the talus bone in the foot.

When you bend your knees while standing upright, your lower legs also hinge forward over the feet at the ankle joints.

Springy feet. The front half of each foot has long thin bones like the fingers. The back half is made up of tarsals, a group of asymmetrical bones including the calcaneus (heel bone) and talus, mentioned above.

The joints between the talus and calcaneus allow the foot

to move side to side on the leg. While sitting, rotate your feet, wiggle your toes, and notice the wide range of motions you have available.

Many of us imagine that our feet stick out from our legs, forming a capital L. In truth, the strong calcaneus extends behind the ankle in each foot, forming part of the outer arch that supports the leg bones from its center. Our feet have three arches: the familiar inner arch, a parallel outer arch, and a transverse arch across the foot. They yield gracefully to our weight and spring back each time we take a step.

While standing, slowly lean your weight more to the inner sides of your feet, and then more to the outside. Rock forward toward your toes, and back toward your heels. What feels most familiar? Where do you feel the most support and connection to the earth? Experiment with placing your feet differently as you move around.

Power. Our legs and feet give us the power to change our location, defend ourselves, and dance for joy. To survive, we sometimes have to suppress that power. To thrive, we slowly reconnect with our legs and enjoy the power they give us. If our leg motion is limited, our body finds other ways to dance, kick, and run.

Protect Your Irritated Nervous System

Your nervous system interprets sensations and enables actions. It is made up of the brain and spinal cord, as well as a branching network of nerves throughout the body. Your nervous system constantly transmits electrical and biochemical signals back and forth between your brain and the rest of your body.

Physical irritation is defined as inflammation or pain in response to a stimulus. When the nervous system is chronically irritated, it transmits sensations more strongly and is more likely to interpret strong sensations as pain. In addition to pain, the body can interpret irritation as anxiety, frustration, uneasiness, and fear.

Awareness of irritation. An important technique in CranioSacral Therapy is to move in the direction of ease. If a client's neck turns more easily to the left, we move it to the left first. The body relaxes because the motion is familiar. At the same time, movement brings heightened awareness to tension patterns that prevent turning to the right. After moving in the direction of ease, gentle movement in the opposite direction becomes possible, and the range of motion increases.

Similarly, becoming aware of irritation can be easier than seeking calm. We become aware of our responses to increased irritation, which gives us information about how it might feel to be less irritated. With gentle humor, we can acknowledge the ways we unintentionally increase our exposure to irritants.

Accumulated stress. An innately sensitive nervous system becomes irritated more quickly. A more insulated system can handle more stress with equanimity, but it also has its limits. Difficult life experiences, perhaps outright trauma or perhaps the "normal" stress of the modern harried lifestyle, consume our tolerance for stress. When our nervous system is overwhelmed, it stores experiences until the resources are available to process them. The stored experiences act as hidden irritants to our systems.

We often push ourselves to stay in irritating environments, ignoring symptoms of sensitivities to foods, chemicals, or noise, and using addictions or dissociation to deaden our responses. We may not recognize that the environment is causing a problem, or we may need something the environment provides, or we might not yet realize we can choose to protect ourselves.

When you notice that an environment is irritating for your system, take breaks or try to tone down intense stimulation. Be mindful of the trade-off between what you get from the environment, and what it costs you to be there.

Denied experience. Denial is a useful survival tool to slow overwhelming change. It shades into self-gaslighting when our internal doubts constantly question our perceptions. The ongoing conflict between direct sensory perception and contradictory beliefs acts like sandpaper on the nervous system.

Almost all of us unconsciously deny our physical experience through our inaccurate internal maps of our bodies, as discussed in the rest of this Body section.

As you learn more about your body map, your nervous system receives more congruent feedback, which is less irritating. For example, many of us are not aware that the heel is not directly under the ankle, but behind it by a couple of inches. Touch your heel and the knobs above your ankle to check. Rock your foot at the ankle and feel where the movement occurs. How does your body respond when you attend to your present experience?

Relentless criticism. When our Inner Critic has free rein to tell us everything that is wrong and bad about ourselves, we become steeped in shame. We blame ourselves for everything that goes wrong for ourselves and the people around us, and focus on what we think we should have done differently.

The harder we work to fix ourselves, the less rest the nervous system receives. We might look for someone else to fix our system for us, and continue with their method even if it irritates our system further. When we give ourselves permission to be imperfect, we can back away from treatments that our system cannot tolerate.

Social boundaries. We all have people who get on our last nerve. Perhaps they blame, criticize, doubt, and undermine us, or perhaps they trigger us in some way. At times we allow our commitments to other people or organizations to take priority over our health.

When we feel invaded, sometimes we tell ourselves we are too defensive instead of asserting our boundaries. Over time, we can take action to protect ourselves even when our concerns seem "silly" to ourselves or others.

Gain awareness. Physical and emotional pain can be both a symptom of irritation and a direct cause of further irritation. You might reflexively respond to pain with denial, self-criticism, and efforts to fix it, making it even more powerful as an irritant.

As you gain awareness of the ways your nervous system responds to irritants, you can make informed choices about allowing additional irritants in your life. Over time, you can interrupt cycles of pain and add gentle motion in the direction of calmness with self-compassion, support, and protective boundaries.

Resources

The first half of Liz Koch's *Core Awareness: Enhancing Yoga, Pilates, Exercise, and Dance,* North Atlantic Books, 2012, describes her metaphorical discoveries about the psoas and its role in the body. The second half contains detailed instructions, including photos, for explorations toward awareness of the psoas and inner core.

Eight Steps to a Pain-Free Back: Remember When It Didn't Hurt, Independent Publishers Group, 2008, by Esther Gokhale carefully describes new ways of sitting and standing to help stretch and relax your back.

Barbara Conable's *What Every Musician Needs to Know About the Body: The Practical Application Of Body Mapping To Making Music,* Andover Press, 2000, a playful, engaging guide to exploring an accurate body map, should be called "What Every Human Needs to Know About the Body."

Barbara Conable's *How to Learn the Alexander Technique: A Manual for Students,* Andover Press, 1995, is a compassionate, accurate manual on how to move human bodies. It is useful for all humans, not just Alexander students.

In *My Body Politic: A Memoir,* University of Michigan Press, 2007, Simi Linton discusses her vibrant career, relationships, and activism as a disabled woman after a car crash paralyzed her legs.

4: Trauma Effects

Even though we work for years to be more present in our bodies and protect our health, we cannot erase all the physical and emotional effects of our trauma histories. Instead of seeing continuing effects as a weakness or failure, we could see them as reassuring physical proof that something happened.

Trauma effects remind us that we deserve gentle care from ourselves and others. As you read this section, remember to pause occasionally to sense whether you feel overwhelmed and need a break.

An acute traumatic event such as a car crash or rape

disrupts our sense of safety in the world, and might leave the body caught in an interrupted fight, flight, or freeze reaction. Over time, Post-Traumatic Stress Disorder (PTSD) symptoms improve through reconnecting with present resources, incrementally processing the event, and helping the body understand that the emergency is over.

Trauma can also be ongoing, such as domestic violence, child sexual abuse, or military service. As well as overwhelming our available resources, ongoing trauma adds the inability to get away, as well as the likelihood of getting survival needs met by the same people who are inflicting harm. Ongoing trauma disrupts our fundamental sense of who we are, where we belong, and how we relate to others. This fundamental disruption, known as Complex PTSD, is primarily a relational wound. It heals as we gather positive experiences in relationship with others, gradually.

Developmental trauma, ongoing violation and/or abandonment by trusted people during childhood, is as much about what was missing as about what happened. Chronically traumatized children focus on survival, not learning. Healing from a traumatic childhood includes picking up missing physical skills such as relaxing, resting, and falling asleep easily, as well as missing social skills such as recognizing trustworthy people and relating to them. Traumatized adults may also need to relearn these skills.

Any trauma can disrupt social bonds when people choose to side with an abuser or back away from someone in pain.

Even though we might feel better most of the time, we will occasionally fall into a hole of old memories, emotions, and patterns. With Complex PTSD and developmental trauma, additional layers of painful memories can continue to surface after years of work.

Not Alone with Your ACEs

The ACE Study* looks at the correlation between **Adverse Childhood Experiences** (ACEs) and health. Between 1995 and 1997, 17,000 middle-income, college-educated adults with access to good health care in the United States joined the study. They had a standardized physical exam and filled out a confidential survey with questions about childhood maltreatment and family dysfunction, as well as current health status and behaviors.

While the ACE Study continues to track the health of participants, there are already major findings.

- Almost two-thirds of study participants had at least one ACE, and more than one in five reported three or more ACEs.

- As the number of ACEs increases, the risk of chronic illness, risky behaviors, and suicide attempts also increases. The correlation is as strong as the correlation between unprotected sex and pregnancy. Chronic toxic stress affects a child's growing brain and body in consistent, predictable ways.

You can check your ACE score with the 10 questions in

---

* "Relationship of Childhood Abuse and Household Dysfunction to Many of the Leading Causes of Death in Adults ", Felitti, Vincent J. et al., American Journal of Preventive Medicine , Volume 14 , Issue 4 , 245 - 258
ajpmonline.org/article/S0749-3797(98)00017-8/pdf

Appendix 1, page 271.

You can also think about factors that helped you be more resilient. We each have protective factors that helped us survive. Our bodies find ways to manage chronic stress. We find nurturing allies, and ways to be self-nurturing. Families hand down strategies for survival.

Part of the majority. People who experienced childhood trauma tend to feel alone and abnormal. Society's message is that we should be strong enough to overcome trauma's effects, and we should definitely avoid impinging on anyone else. Illness and dysfunction are viewed as the individual's fault, and the individual's responsibility to fix.

In fact, a large majority of people experience significant childhood trauma, making it sadly "normal." The effects are real and profound. This is a social and medical crisis that requires more than individual resources to address.

Trauma-informed care. Pediatrician Nadine Burke Harris founded the Center for Youth Wellness, where they use the ACE study information to directly help patients. They screen children for adverse experiences and intervene with home visits, education, psychotherapy, mindfulness and coping skills, and referrals to other practitioners. Her TED talk* is a great summary of the effects of Adverse Childhood Experiences and her work to help people heal.

Imagine if we all had such comprehensive trauma-informed support as children and adults.

We are allowed to be affected. We are allowed to have fibromyalgia, chronic fatigue, environmental sensitivities,

---

* Nadine Burke Harris, "How Childhood Trauma Affects Health Across a Lifetime"
ted.com/talks/nadine_burke_harris_how_childhood_trauma_affects_health_across_a_lifetime

digestive issues, anxiety, depression, and PTSD.

We are allowed to have heart disease, diabetes, and other illnesses that are falsely labeled "lifestyle" diseases. Our bodies are allowed to be heavier, which is not a sign of ill health in itself.

We are allowed to try to regulate our irritated nervous systems with substances both legal and illegal. We are allowed to have troubled relationships. We are allowed to have a seemingly bottomless well of need inside for comforting and love.

We are allowed to be perfectionists and drive ourselves fiercely to success after success. We are allowed to work desperately hard at healing.

Responsive to treatment. Fortunately, the brain and body remain responsive past childhood, so we can mitigate the effects of chronic stress. We can meditate. We can seek out caring, kind people both professionally and personally. We can write and draw our stories. We can allow our emotions time and space to emerge. We can spend time outside, and gently move our bodies.

If we have money and access to well-supplied grocery stores, we can buy food that puts less stress on our bodies. If we have money and access to healers, we can get trauma-informed bodywork and psychotherapy. If we have health insurance and money, we can get medical treatment.

With the United States social structure and medical system, people with less privilege are more likely to grow up in traumatic circumstances and less likely to have access to effective care. The effects of trauma are more likely to be seen as personal failings, rather than physical consequences of Adverse Childhood Experiences.

Kindness and understanding. The most powerful action

we can take is to stop blaming ourselves and others for misfortune, illness, and struggle. We have the bodies we have, unfairly marked by past trauma. We can start where we are, and treat ourselves with kindness and understanding as we heal.

Name Memories Without Words

Infants are born with survival drives to learn about the world, and to bond with their carers. They absorb information with their whole bodies, gathering sensory impressions and learning basic skills of responsiveness and movement. Physical and relational lessons learned in infancy inform every moment of our lives.

Infant nervous systems are not yet fully formed and lack the capacity to self-regulate. Infants depend on their carers to directly soothe their nervous systems and to teach by example how to soothe themselves and return to calm after an emotional or physical disturbance.

Secure attachment. When all goes well, a carer (the mother or father, or another adult, or an older child) responds to a baby with loving eye contact, open delight in her explorations, concern and soothing for distress, and respect for her rhythms of connection and space. The baby learns with her whole body that she is successful at bonding, and her needs will be met. Her self is cradled in welcoming arms and nourished by loving reflections from the people around her.

Carers do not have to be perfect to provide secure attachment. A "good enough" carer attunes to the baby most of the time, and responds to attempts to repair the connection when attunement is disrupted.

Insecure attachment strategies. To a baby, lack of welcome or even a brief abandonment is a threat to survival. Experiments have consistently shown three different responses to care that is not "good enough": avoidant, ambivalent, and disorganized attachment strategies. Attachment strategies tend to be stable through a person's life and deeply affect relationships and happiness.

Avoidant attachment. If carers are consistently unresponsive but not otherwise threatening, the baby withdraws her confident expectation that her needs will be met. She learns to rely only on herself rather than reaching out for connection.

At first, babies cry for attention. If left alone for too long or too often without a response, they fall into silent resignation and despair. They might appear quietly well-behaved, at the cost of a huge wound to the spirit.

Ambivalent attachment. If carers are sometimes responsive and sometimes unreachable, the baby learns that care is dependent on certain behaviors, rather than being her birthright.

The growing child attunes to her carers, trying desperately to discern how to get care, rather than receiving the carers' attunement. The behaviors she settles on are intermittently reinforced, since the carers are responding to forces outside the child's control.

Disorganized attachment. Sometimes carers are actively threatening, a source of terror as well as care. The baby's nervous system is thrown into unresolvable conflict between the powerful need to flee, and the equally powerful need to move toward safety.

The baby might dissociate to contain the contradiction, a tearing dis-integration of consciousness from the body, with the wordless sense that this should not be happening, and the world is unutterably hostile and dangerous.

Intact need to connect. The drive to bond remains intact beneath insecure attachment strategies. It is possible to acquire "earned secure attachment" by processing negative early experiences and mindfully entering into a "good enough" relationship in the present. The relationship can be with an empathic friend, partner, family member, or therapist who can provide a strong container for memories that come up.

Preverbal flashbacks can be triggered by conflict between the need to connect and the bone-deep memory of abandonment. Reaching out for support that feels safe, taking tiny risks and evaluating the results, and making a lot of space for difficult feelings can help move through the painful healing process.

Intensity from the past. Flashbacks to preverbal memories are intense, all-consuming, boundaryless. The body feeling might be raw terror, or blank detachment, or inconsolable despair. The world feels huge, overwhelming, unmanageable. There is a sense of fundamental helplessness, failure to connect, inability to reach safety. With all of itself, the body demands to be held, rescued, enfolded in care.

If you have felt that way before, it helps to gather a set of first-aid phrases and actions for when it happens again. Retreat under the covers, drink warm tea, call a reliable friend. Whatever helps you get through.

It can take the edge off preverbal flashbacks to recognize that intense feelings might belong to the past rather than the present. At first that might be easier once the storm has passed. With time, the intensity itself becomes a familiar cue, the way "always", "never", and "forever" are flashback markers.

When an extreme emotional experience does not obviously connect to the present and is difficult to describe in words, check inside if it might be old. The response might be a sense of easing, or a deep breath, or a feeling of rightness. The response might also include a sense of what is triggering in the present. The recognition gives a sliver of breathing room, a place to stand and witness.

Gentle touch. Gentle steady physical contact tells the body in its own language that the nightmare ended and it is safe now to expand into life rather than contract against it. The touch can come from a trusted person, or a pet, or your own hand on belly or heart. Listen inside for what your body needs. It might be whispering, or loudly demanding.

Witness, find words. Witness and express your experience. You might start with sounds, like whimpering, and motions, like curling up small. Begin to find words for the edges of your experience, from the outside looking in. Keep describing, and checking with the wordlessness, and refining the description.

You might get images or impressions of a narrative behind the intense emotions. Consider accepting the narrative as your truth, even though we think "babies don't remember" and "no one would do that to a baby." Our personal truth does not need to be proven in a court of law, and babies do remember, and unfortunately some people perpetrate horrific physical, sexual, and emotional abuse on babies.

Protection and care. All babies invite and deserve protection, care, and love, including you. If that does not feel self-evidently true, it might be time to build secure attachment with yourself. Listen with kind attentiveness to your sensations, emotions, preferences, and needs, especially the ones that seem "unreasonable." Move toward what feels nourishing and healing. Protect yourself fiercely from harm. You deserve attunement and connection.

Safety in Your Bones

You are deep in conversation when someone unexpectedly taps your shoulder from behind. What do you do?

- Turn calmly to see who it is.
- Duck away from the touch.
- Turn sharply and grab the hand.
- That would never happen because you always have your back to a wall.

Someone who feels safe and relaxed is likely to turn calmly. Ducking or grabbing the hand are examples of startle responses from an activated nervous system. With mild hypervigilance, unexpected events are interpreted as threats. With strong hypervigilance, threats are expected and prepared for, such as keeping one's back to a wall.

Preparation for danger. Hypervigilance is a primary symptom of Post-Traumatic Stress Disorder (PTSD). Both consciously and unconsciously, after trauma it is natural to think, "I didn't like how that went. If I don't relax, I can keep terrible things from happening." Muscles stay tense in an ongoing effort to prepare for danger.

In truth, feeling safe did not cause the traumatic event, and relaxed alertness is the best starting point to handle unexpected problems. When the cycle of nervous system activation and settling is complete after trauma, we naturally return to relaxed alertness. If the process of trembling and release is interrupted, we remain tense and jumpy, sometimes for years.

Trauma survivors often try to control the external environment to make it safe enough, or become resigned to always feeling unsafe. Victim-blaming contributes to this by telling us that it is the victim's responsibility to notice danger and take action to avoid it. While awareness of red flags can sometimes help us detect danger, victims are not to blame for experiencing trauma.

Childhood safety. If all goes well, children internalize a sense of safety within the contained environment maintained by parents and other caregivers. The wider world is uncertain, but the child is protected from danger and provided with both physical and emotional resources. The growing child alternates between exploration and retreat, risk and protection.

Many of us lacked childhood safety or lost it too early. As adults, we long for someone to protect and provide for us, unaware of other options to feel safe. We may also carry the remembered imprint of a small child who, surrounded by indifferent or hostile giants, decided that safety is impossible.

Safety as a guarantee. Those who have never experienced trauma, or who have buried all awareness of it, can easily believe that their choices and divine intervention have kept them safe. They define safety as a guarantee that nothing harmful will happen. Trauma shatters this innocent belief, requiring survivors to renegotiate their faith as well as a new definition of safety.

Safety as confidence and resilience. Safety is an internal experience of confidence and resilience in relation to the environment. An environment that one person experiences as unsafe and overwhelming, for example slippery ice with people rushing in all directions, might be safe and even delightful for an experienced ice skater on a rink.

One aspect of safety is tolerance for mistakes and uncertainty. Experienced skaters know they can handle a fall, so they can risk trying new moves.

Take a few minutes to notice what safety means to you. Is it something you long for, take for granted, seek out, or gave up on? What qualities in an environment help you feel confident and resilient?

Absence of threat. One reason survivors struggle to feel safe after trauma is the difficulty of proving the absence of threat. Even when the environment seems safe, an old danger could reappear or a new one fall from the sky at any moment. Take some time to sense your current environment. Does it present a physical or emotional threat right now? What tools do you have in the present to handle a sudden threat? Do you trust your body to mobilize as soon as a threat appears? Can you imagine resting in the absence of an immediate threat?

Relax to feel safe. The brain can interpret long-term chronic tension as a sign of a threat, so sometimes we have to relax to feel safe, rather than feel safe to relax.

How would you sit, stand, and move differently if you felt safe? Imagine that you are protected and provided for, at least for a moment. How would it feel to be a cat sprawled in a sunbeam in the middle of the floor, completely unguarded?

Commanding ourselves to relax can be counter-productive when we criticize ourselves for being tense. Here are two experiments that can lead to more relaxation.

Experiment 1: Let go of your bones. Bring your attention to your upper arm just below the shoulder, and imagine the muscles giving your humerus (upper arm bone, see figure, page 98) a little more space all the way around. Find another place in your body that you feel connected to and try letting go of the bones there, too. Notice what happens, whether it is a deep breath, a sense of space, increased tension, or an inability to feel anything.

Experiment 2: Rest your shoulders on your ribs and spine. Our shoulders often hunch toward our ears to brace against possible threats. Small neck muscles work hard to pull up the whole shoulder girdle, made up of shoulder blades, collar bones, and arms (see figure, page 98). The shoulders and arms are designed to be supported by the rib cage and spine. Can you imagine your shoulder blades resting comfortably on your ribs? Can you imagine your arms resting downward, fully supported? Again, notice what happens.

A skill and a choice. Safety is an internal experience, a skill to be learned and a choice to be made. In the end, you just have to try it. In the absence of immediate threats, consider allowing yourself to feel safe, just for a moment.

Rest at Sleep's Threshold

Lack of safety can make it hard to sleep. Disturbed sleep is a major symptom of Post-Traumatic Stress Disorder (PTSD). Traumatized people struggle with the transitions into and out of sleep, as well as with nightmares that can be traumatic in themselves. Lack of sleep further destabilizes the nervous system, making it harder to cope with and heal from other effects of trauma.

Trying to fall asleep with PTSD can feel like edging carefully between an ocean of flashbacks and a cliff of sleeplessness. The ongoing sense of emergency creates physical tension and racing thoughts. Relaxing feels like letting down a necessary guard against outer threats and inner revelations.

Getting up in the morning can also be a difficult journey, shaking off nightmares in preparation for another day. Transitions are hard, especially when they involve vulnerability.

Time for rest. Whether you sleep or not, night can be a time for rest, contemplation, and listening inside. You might be sleeping more than you think, micro-naps with dreams that continue where wakefulness left off. As a passenger on a long car trip, I once dreamed that I was lying awake in bed.

It can take time for the underlying irritated nervous system to calm down, and to find what sleep conditions work best for you. Meanwhile, simple interventions can ease nightmares and alleviate the extra layer of anxiety about not sleeping well.

Acknowledge what is. The first step is to acknowledge the current situation with sleep, both positive and negative. Perhaps you fall asleep easily, even if you wake often during the night. Perhaps you have chronic insomnia at night, but find time for refreshing naps. Perhaps your sleep is frustratingly rare and fragmented, and yet you still find ways to move through your days.

Encourage sleep. Become mindful about your relationship with sleep and the factors that affect it. When is your sleep better and worse? Experiment to see what works best for you. Some people find the recommendations of sleep hygiene helpful, which include a regular bedtime and wake time, a quiet, dark room, and only staying in bed for sleep.

Not everyone has control over their schedule or sleep environment. Some people find that reading or checking email in bed helps with the transitions into and out of sleep. Listening to familiar music at bedtime can help calm the nervous system for sleep. Earplugs might shield against noise, or they might feel like reckless interference with sensing for danger. For some people, small amounts of caffeine keep them up for hours, while for others caffeine acts as a sedative. The key is to make informed choices and understand how they affect you.

Sleep aids. A soothing drink at bedtime such as chamomile or valerian tea can help prepare your body for sleep. Melatonin can help regulate your sleep/wake cycles. Over-the-counter or prescription sedatives can bring relief when sleep is out of reach. A doctor can also check into the possibility of sleep apnea or other treatable medical conditions.

Orient to the present. Survivors of sexual assault may still wake suddenly at the time of night the assault(s) occurred, or "inexplicably" resist going to bed until after that time. Beds and bedrooms may feel triggering and unsafe, the opposite of a safe haven. Combat veterans and other survivors of violent trauma often sleep lightly and wake suddenly in response to noise.

When awakened suddenly, orient yourself to the present by reminding yourself where you are and what the date is. It might help to turn on the light and look around, or have a night light you can focus on.

Remind yourself that it ended and you are not confronting an emergency in this moment. The body insistently reviews past trauma, searching for resolution. Each spike of anxiety and return to calm reminds you that resolution already occurred.

Connect with your body. Whether you have been startled awake or cannot fall asleep, it is natural to respond with frustration at yourself and the situation. Take some time to notice your physical and emotional responses, and say hello to them.

- Hello, quickly beating heart.
- Hello, something in me angry at noisy people.
- Hello, something in me ashamed of what happened decades ago.

Feel breath flowing in and out of your body. Notice the support of your bed, and how your body responds to it. Say hello to any tension you notice in your shoulders, or in your jaw. Wiggle your fingers and toes, and notice your adult length, here in bed, in the present.

Listen for requests. Is there anything that could be more comfortable? Hold the question gently, and sense for answers that float up. They might be new and unexpected, or part of an ongoing theme. You might want more light, or thicker curtains. Something to eat or drink. More blankets, or fewer. A different pillow. To get up and write (but not send) a scathing letter. To stop thinking about that problem entirely for a while.

Receive the answers with openness, and let them know you hear them. As a separate step decide whether to take any action. It can be hard to get out of bed in the middle of the night, even if it would be easier to go to sleep afterward. Perhaps something in you needs reminding that adults are allowed to get up when it suits them.

Some sleep environment issues can be addressed with others during the day. Whether it's a neighbor gardening at 5am, a housemate slamming doors, or a loudly beeping garbage truck, people respond surprisingly well to a polite request tinged with desperation for sleep.

Nightmares. Nightmares make sleep less restful, and add dread to the thought of going to sleep. They can be ever-changing scenes with an emotional punch of helplessness and terror, repetitive flashbacks to trauma, or a tangle of both.

Script your dreams. Anne Germain's research on Imagery Scripting* shows that imagining (not just thinking about) what you want to dream can replace nightmares with more pleasant dreams.

Either imagine a better ending for a repeating nightmare, or create a whole new dream. If you start with an existing nightmare, choose one that is upsetting, but not devastating,

---

* Germain A, Nielsen TA. Impact of imagery rehearsal treatment on distressing dreams, psychological distress, and sleep parameters in nightmare patients. Behavioral Sleep Medicine, 1:140-154, 2003

to keep this process manageable. Have fun with scripting your new dream. What would be a wonderful, delightful outcome? How do you want to feel when you wake up?

One possibility is to imagine that a guardian comes into your dreams to protect you. The guardian could be God, Kuan Yin, your older brother, an imaginary aunt, or your favorite superhero. Vividly imagine your caring, competent guardian standing ready to take action on your behalf. Feel their warm presence supporting you.

Close your eyes and imagine your new dream. Make it as dreamlike and vivid as possible, using all your senses. Practice at least once a day, more if possible.

Practical action. Difficulties with sleep can reinforce feelings of helplessness and powerlessness from the past. When we can acknowledge our present reality, explore how to encourage sleep, advocate for ourselves, and re-script our nightmares, we reinforce present resourcefulness in place of past helplessness.

Exit Emergency Mode

Emergencies are loud, intense, exciting, chaotic. They demand our full, focused attention. When survival is at stake, there is no time for rest, repair, or pause for thought. The body goes into debt for energy, sleep, and nutrients, planning to make it up after the emergency is over.

Ongoing emergency. The essence of Post-Traumatic Stress Disorder (PTSD) is a continuing state of emergency after surviving the initial trauma. The body has not yet received the news that safety is restored, and insists, "Do something!" even when there is nothing immediate to do.

Emergency Mode can manifest as ongoing anxiety about current problems. When the nervous system is already on high alert, it tinges everything with urgency and panic. When the nervous system calms down, current issues can shrink from huge obstacles to manageable annoyances.

Unrecognized safety. We may long for peace, but not recognize or adapt to it when it arrives. Infant nervous systems learn calmness from surrounding adults. When children grow up surrounded by people in Emergency Mode, they miss learning how safety feels. The lack of an emergency feels like an absence, another problem to be solved, rather than the presence of quiet.

You are already enough. In Emergency Mode, our Inner Critic monitors and corrects our behavior to keep us safe. The Inner Critic barks commands because in an emergency it seems there is no time to be gentle or kind. We try to get out of Emergency Mode by criticizing ourselves and commanding ourselves to relax, intensifying the problem.

In contrast to the Inner Critic's approach, find an exit from Emergency Mode by creating space to be exactly who you are right now. You do not have to become someone else to survive.

Connect with your sense of urgency. To find calmness, make contact with your sense of urgency, without allowing it to take over. Take your time to describe how it feels in this moment.

- Something in me feels like I can't sit still.
- Something in me feels braced for disaster.
- Something in me believes I'm barely making it.
- Something in me is always terrified.

As you find words or images, also notice where the sensation lives in your body. Say a gentle hello to anything you notice.

Sense the present. If the sense of urgency becomes overwhelming, consciously notice your present surroundings. Out loud, name what you see, hear, and sense. Ask yourself if you are in physical danger in this moment. Feel your breath moving through your body. You are alive. You are surviving.

Remind yourself that you made it through emergencies in the past and have more resources now. You have an adult's size, strength, and skills, and each year brings more wisdom and experience. Push down through your heels to feel your length, and push out through your elbows to feel your width.

Give urgency more room. If your sense of urgency is contained in a small area of your body, try allowing it more room. Start with a small increase. Paradoxically, emotions are usually less overwhelming if they can move through a larger space. Many of us formed our strategies for handling overwhelming emotions as physically tiny toddlers. As adults, we have a much larger capacity available.

Already solved. If a current problem feels insurmountable, take some time to acknowledge your specific feelings around the problem. Gently ask if any of these are old feelings, echoes of old emergencies. What if the emergency is over?

When we are caught up in Emergency Mode, we overlook possible solutions to current problems. Make a list of ways you could reach out for help. Even if you choose not to do any of them, it helps you remember your available options.

Ask yourself, "What if this problem is already solved?" In that alternate reality, how would you feel? What would you be doing? What if you truly do not need to take any action?

You might find that you can put the problem down for now. You might find that unexpected solutions pop into your head. Your body might continue to insist, "Danger! Danger!" Ask yourself if there is any action that feels self-protective in the moment. Whether the sense of danger is from the past or present, you do not have to ignore it or push it away.

Reduce irritants. Is your physical environment irritating your nervous system and contributing to a sense of emergency? Notice your sensitivities and avoid them when you can. As you move toward a calmer environment both internally and externally, your body will more easily exit Emergency Mode.

As Julia Ross describes in *The Mood Cure,* long-term Emergency Mode can deplete the body of nutrients. Supplements can support recovery by replenishing depleted stores.

Take time to be kind. Emergency Mode can increase our defensiveness when survival feels threatened, and can cause conflict if someone disagrees that a problem is urgent. Keep in mind that each nervous system evaluates a situation based on individual past history and current resources. Even in an emergency, take time to be kind, both to others and yourself.

Subtle progress. You might experience a dramatic exit from Emergency Mode if your body suddenly notices, "Oh, you're right, the emergency is over!" More likely, you will notice subtle shifts at first, where you feel less desperate less often, and recover a little more quickly from unpleasant surprises. Instead of questioning your perceptions as false hope, gather your subtle signs of progress and believe that you have rounded the corner.

Triggered! Now What?

A scent wafts by, or someone speaks certain words in a certain tone, or that time of year comes around again. Suddenly we are defiantly thirteen, or playfully four, or speechlessly afraid in situations where we would prefer to be competent adults.

With awareness, we might be able to take back adult control, or we might just get through the moment as best we can, hoping no one notices. The sense of being hijacked might be familiar, or this might be the first time a buried part has surfaced in recent memory. While our system is flooded, our usual creativity, flexibility, and problem-solving abilities are physiologically unavailable. We can reach for our basic survival tools, breathe, look around, and remind ourselves that the triggering will end.

Everyone gets triggered. Later, we might scheme to release that errant part so it cannot embarrass us again, thinking of that as healing and resolving to work harder at it. We often see regressing or switching to a younger part as a failure, as if we "should" have our best adult faculties available at all times. This is a subtle form of victim-blaming, where any weakness, faltering, or vulnerability is seen as a reason to be hurt.

It may be more obvious when someone with PTSD gets triggered, but it happens to everyone. We behave more warmly toward a stranger who happens to look like our beloved third-grade teacher. We refuse to eat anything with peanut butter after a food poisoning incident. The past weaves through our present, shaping our reactions far more than we consciously realize.

Allow closeness. The simple but not easy process of healing is to allow those younger parts to come closer, rather than pushing them away. Each one got left behind, frozen in time, because of overwhelming events. Our responses to the young parts echo our responses back then, including dissociation, fear, shame, rage, and a need to fix it right now.

Turn toward resistance. Even when we know that acceptance is the key to feeling better, our resistant responses need to be acknowledged and given time first. We can say hello to the part who wants nothing to do with frightened or playful inner children, who is concerned with surviving in the present, who may, given spacious attention, reveal a panicked need to flee that comes from the past.

From that place of spacious listening, we can let the panicky part know that it makes sense it would feel that way, given what was happening back then, and it gets to feel that way as long as it wants.

We can also gently take note of what has changed since then, taking in the present environment. Perhaps it is safer now than it was then to be vulnerable, or perhaps there are good reasons for continuing wariness. Most importantly, that old situation ended, and we have new skills and new possibilities now.

Hear what they know. To allow younger parts to come closer, we have to be willing to hear and feel what they know. They might carry traumatic memories in the form of images, emotions, or body sensations. They might carry love for an abuser. They might carry awareness of body parts that have long been dissociated and numb, like the pelvis.

Simply acknowledge. Eventually, something shifts inside and we give our consent to know. The new information might slide silently into place, or come in flashes, or approach and withdraw as the younger part gains trust. It might crash against us in waves until something deeper shifts in our understanding of the present or the past. We might feel calm, or numb, or overwhelmed with emotion. We might ruefully acknowledge that it made sense to resist.

Even though we might want to fix the past problem, offer comfort, or change the younger part's experience, all we need to do is acknowledge the information we received. "I see that image, feel that emotion, acknowledge the love, sense my pelvis." We can also acknowledge our reactions to the new information. For example, it is common to feel shame for positive feelings toward abusers, even though capacity for love is cause for celebration, not shame.

Blending skills. Once a connection is made with a younger part, information flows both ways. They can look around at the present and see that it is different from the past. They see the skills and strengths and wisdom we have acquired in the intervening years and tentatively try new ways of being in the world. The next time they take over, adult and child can blend together, with access to more inner resources.

The younger part may express needs or longings or fears that affect present-day actions. At first, we can declare a Decision-Free Zone and simply listen. Over time, we incorporate their wishes into our actions, neither ignoring them nor letting them take over.

Time for repair. When we believe we have everything under control, being triggered can be a frustrating and embarrassing interruption. It reminds us that we are fallible, vulnerable, and affected by the past. While we might expect ourselves to be in top form at all times, getting triggered reminds us that we need time to rest, regroup, and repair past injuries.

Effects of Sexual Assault

Reading about sexual assault can be triggering for survivors. If you find yourself feeling overwhelmed or dissociated, give yourself kind permission to take a break and do something you enjoy. This article describes effects of sexual assault, not assaults themselves.

Responses to sexual assault range from severe trauma to shrugging it off. If you have been sexually assaulted, you may have some, none, or all of the effects mentioned below. All your experiences and responses are valid. If you have some of these effects with no memory of sexual assault, that is also valid. You are the authority on your history.

Sexual assault includes rape, incest, and other forms of sexual touching without consent. Perpetrators assault people of all genders and all ages. It is a crime of violence and power, not passion or lack of self-control.

Boundary violation. Sexual assault ruptures personal boundaries. The perpetrator says, "What you want doesn't matter. Your wholeness has no value to me. Your personhood is erased." The victim has an internal experience of invalidation and violation of self, causing profound grief. "This is not what I wanted."

Victim-blaming. Sexual assault is one of the few crimes where the victim is put on trial more than the perpetrator. Instead of offering support, community members often engage in denial and hostile interrogation. "You imagined it." "You misunderstood." "You invited it."

This gaslighting undermines survivors' self-trust. While healing from an external attack, survivors also fight an internal battle for their own truth in the face of denial, confusion, and pressure to consider themselves less important than the perpetrator. Many perpetrators create plausible deniability through alcohol, manipulation, and brazen lies.

Betrayal. Contrary to the image of being assaulted by a stranger in a dark alley, the perpetrator is often known to the victim. Many perpetrators intentionally build trust before an assault, or take advantage of existing relationships such as within a family, school, workplace, or religious organization.

Sexual assault diminishes survivors' sense of safety in their world. Assault by a stranger brings fear that it will happen again in that location or anywhere. Assault by a known person shatters trust in that person and damages survivors' connections with surrounding community. Whether the survivor remains silent, confronts the perpetrator, or tells others, relationships are lost and altered.

Ongoing interaction. When community members refuse to choose sides in the name of false "fairness," the victim has to do the work to avoid further interactions with the perpetrator, if avoidance is possible. When perpetrators are family members, coworkers, fellow soldiers, or influential community members, it requires radical life changes to avoid them.

Dissociation from the body. Like any trauma, sexual assault can cause PTSD and general dissociation. In addition, it can cause toxic body shame and dissociation from affected parts, especially the pelvis. Survivors may perceive their bodies as fragmented pieces rather than one whole. Many survivors blame their bodies and physical responses for the assault, rather than placing appropriate blame on the perpetrator.

It becomes more difficult to be fully present, causing loss of both skill and enjoyment in physical activities. Survivors may avoid medical care, which is often invasive and rushed rather than compassionate.

Disrupted sexuality. Instead of connection and pleasure, sexual feelings become associated with objectification and pain. Sexual feelings may be avoided entirely or pursued obsessively. Sexually assaulted children lose the opportunity to develop their sexuality at their own pace as they mature.

Perceived loss of value. Society attaches value to people's sexual status. Women "should" be virgins or monogamously married. Men "should" not be penetrated. Children "should" be innocent. Victims of sexual assault feel shame not just because of gaslighting and confusion, but also because they internalize society's condemnation as "damaged goods."

Survivors feel shame for not resisting enough, for not avoiding the rapist, for somehow "inviting" the assault. The perpetrator is the one who should feel ashamed, along with anyone who tries to shame the survivor.

Evaluating people on their sexual status objectifies them, and blaming people for a crime committed against them is the essence of injustice. Everyone deserves respect and approval irrelevant of their sexual status.

Pregnancy and children. Some rapes result in pregnancy. The survivor may not have access to abortion, or may choose to keep the child. All the physical, psychological, and social effects of rape intrude on the parent-child bond before and after birth. In some situations, the rapist may be able to claim parental rights, intruding even more on the survivor's life. Children born of incest from a close genetic relative have a higher risk of genetic abnormalities. When the innocent child resembles the rapist, it adds an extra layer of suffering. After being raped during the Rwandan genocide, a mother asked, "Can you tell me how to love my daughter more?"*

End rape culture. Communities are slow to take action against predators in their midst. Confronting perpetrators is hard, especially when they hold positions of power and influence. Lack of community action leaves perpetrators free to continue committing assaults. Rape jokes, sexual objectification, and focusing on prevention by victims rather than perpetrators all support a culture that minimizes and allows rape.

Survivors of sexual assault deserve support, assistance, and care. Most of all, we deserve not to be assaulted. We all deserve a culture that endorses enthusiastic consent, shared power, and zero tolerance for sexual assault.

---

* The New Yorker, "The Legitimate Children of Rape," Andrew Solomon, August 29, 2012
newyorker.com/news/news-desk/the-legitimate-children-of-rape

Relax For Your Life

Content Note: brief child rape example.

Have you held a small child recently? Supported by trusted arms, small children rest with their whole weight, warmly present and relaxed. Over time, many of us lose the ability to relax into support, some gradually, some violently.

During assault. When a rapist commands, "Relax!" the assaulted child understands the message. For survival, do not fight. Do not resist. Go limp. Be silent. The immense energy mobilized for fight or flight is suppressed into surrender. The body's urgent signals of violation and pain are silenced through dissociation.

Aftermath. After a rape, life goes on. Muscle tension holds secret pain and memories at bay. When told to relax, the child dissociates into limp blankness, or looks around to see how others perform relaxation. The deep belief, "I'm wrong, I'm bad," interrupts natural responses.

Now grown, the adult survivor struggles to find a new meaning for "relax." When receiving bodywork, relaxation is supposedly easy and enjoyable, but brings strong emotions and flashbacks instead. Relaxation in social situations is equally puzzling. "Be yourself" is easier without complex secrets to keep or reveal.

Even without assault, a command to "Relax!" is a boundary violation and a red flag. Our internal state is not subject to other people's demands.

Relaxing is not work. Many bodywork clients work hard

to relax, and feel embarrassed or defensive when their arm resists being moved by a practitioner. While bodywork is often relaxing, clients are not required to relax. Forced limpness gets in the way of allowing genuine presence, calmness, and lengthened muscles.

If you find yourself working to relax, bring kind attention to your experience of tension. How does your body interact with the surface supporting you? Are some parts more relaxed than others? How would you describe your sensations? A part might feel braced, withdrawn, defiant, angry, or frightened. Gently inquire, and allow words or images to float into awareness.

Boundary check. Ongoing tension can be a signal that something feels uncomfortable or unsafe. Check in with your boundaries. What needs to change to feel safe?

During bodywork, perhaps you want to keep more clothes on, or avoid touch on your feet, or turn off distracting music. Tracking and expressing your boundaries is an important part of healing. When boundaries are heard and respected, it becomes easier to relax.

Trusted environment. We associate relaxation with safety, trust, and comfort. We breathe a sigh of relief in environments where we feel fully welcome, accepted, and safe from attack.

Remember (or imagine) a time when you felt at ease. Notice your surroundings, and who else is there, if anyone. How does your body feel as you visualize this scene? You might notice warmth, pleasant heaviness in your limbs, a gentle smile, a deeper breath. If you dissociate to relax, you might notice numbness, blankness, or quickly get distracted.

Many people find it difficult to relax without alcohol or

other numbing agents. Anxiety, hypervigilance, or chronic pain can make relaxation feel impossibly distant. Allowing relaxation is a skill that improves with practice.

Trusted self. Not only do we need a trustworthy environment to let down our guard, we need to trust ourselves as well. When we believe there is something wrong with us, we maintain control instead of relaxing. We do not need to try harder, accomplish more, or become better people to deserve relaxation.

Healing can appear to be a difficult, active process to become someone else. While learning new coping skills takes work, much of healing is letting go of all the "shoulds" and relaxing into who we already are.

Internal safe space. Our fierce battles to fix "bad" emotions, memories, and characteristics lock unwanted aspects in place. When we can make room for all aspects of ourselves during internal conflicts, we create a safe space that allows relaxation, movement and change.

We can begin the process with patient listening to the judgmental parts of us who are trying so hard to be "good." Each part gets to be the way it is right now, including the parts that are frustrated with the way things are, until a shift arises organically.

Rest. Relaxation is more subtle than we expect. It has always been there underneath loud tension, quietly awaiting our welcome. Relaxation is surrender, not to someone else, but to our present truth. We release the intense striving to fix what was never broken, return to our first home, the body, after too long away, and rest.

Resources

In *Childhood Disrupted: How Your Biography Becomes Your Biology, and How You Can Heal*, Atria Books, 2016, science journalist Donna Jackson Nakazawa covers the current research on how the brain is changed by toxic stress, and what can be done about it.

The Girls Come Marching Home: Stories of Women Warriors Returning from the War in Iraq, Stackpole Books, 2009, by Kirsten Holmstedt shows both the causes and effects of hypervigilance on women veterans of the war in Iraq, as well as their struggles to feel safe back at home.

The Mood Cure: The 4 Step Program to Take Charge of Your Emotions Today, Penguin Books, 2003, by Julia Ross contains nutritional suggestions to support a calm nervous system.

Naomi Ardea's *The Art of Healing from Sexual Trauma: Tending Body and Soul through Creativity, Nature, and Intuition*, Wise Ink, 2016, is a gentle, supportive, companionable telling of her healing story combined with practical tools for the reader, with luminous art and nature photographs throughout.

Not Trauma Alone: Therapy for Child Abuse Survivors in Family and Social Context, Routledge, 2000, by Steven Gold is a profoundly compassionate, research-based description of the symptoms of Complex PTSD and how to help.

Presence After Trauma

5: Self-Trust

Trauma shatters our trust in the world. Worse, it shatters our trust in ourselves. Encouraged by society's victim-blaming, we hold ourselves responsible for protecting ourselves from abuse and for predicting the future consequences of our choices. We lose trust in our instinct to connect when the people we connect with do us harm.

Over time, we find ways to reconcile with ourselves in the present, working through layers of self-doubt, self-blame, and self-hatred. We get to know ourselves and find ways to accept what we discover. There is always a reason for what we do and how we do it.

We treat ourselves with as much kindness as we can scrape together, starting with acknowledgment of the self-critical voice that is trying to help us survive.

As we accept that trauma occurred and that it was not our fault, we can reestablish trust in our decisions, our resources, our commitments, and our voice. Despite abusive and everyday gaslighting, we rebuild trust in our perceptions, our viewpoint, our wisdom, and our effectiveness in the world.

Permission to Stop Beating Yourself Up

Take a moment to notice your current experience. How do you feel? What thoughts are running through your mind? What sensations does your body report?

Many of us jump directly to evaluation and problem-solving in response to our current experience. We may not be aware of other options, or we may believe constant self-improvement is necessary to measure up. In her book *Self-Compassion*, Kristin Neff proposes kinder responses to both positive and negative experiences.

Self-compassion mantra. Do you notice delight and comfort? Celebrate and savor your enjoyment. Do you notice pain or discomfort? Kristin Neff suggests a mantra for painful moments when something goes wrong or you notice something about yourself you don't like.

This is a moment of suffering.

Suffering is part of life.

May I be kind to myself in this moment.

May I give myself the compassion I need.

The phrases cover three doorways to self-compassion:

- **Mindful awareness.** Awareness helps you take a step back and say, "I am suffering."
- **Shared human experience.** We often feel isolated as part of suffering and imagine that no one else could understand or sympathize with our pain. In truth, everyone suffers in similar ways.

- **Caring concern.** Consider treating yourself the way you would treat a beloved friend. Your Inner Nurturer can help.

The fourth phrase affirms that we are all human beings worthy of compassion in each moment.

You can express the three doorways and the affirmation in your own words. For example, "This is hard. Everyone has hard times. What would a kind friend say right now? Everyone deserves kindness, including me."

No time for that. Your Inner Critic may believe that self-compassion is a luxury or a distraction. Time enough for that after the emergency is over, but the emergency never seems to end. If nothing is going wrong in the present, there is something in the past we should have done better, or something in the future we should figure out how to prevent.

Need to figure it out. Figuring things out is a key survival skill in abusive situations. The ability to recognize patterns and adapt to them is crucial when punishments are arbitrary and cruel. Even in non-abusive situations, figuring things out and fitting in can make life easier. Puzzling social interactions provide endless fodder for self-recrimination and self-improvement.

The problem is that we forget to stop. We continually evaluate our behavior, thoughts, and emotions and usually find ourselves lacking, with brief interludes to celebrate achievements. In an attempt to take responsibility for our lives, we ask ourselves, "What did I do to cause this? What lesson am I supposed to learn? How do I deserve this?" We may not recognize that this constant self-analysis and self-judgment is beating ourselves up.

Past selves on trial. We put our past selves on trial for causing present mishaps, but cause and effect are not so clear. Our actions are woven from genetics, past influences, present environment, physical condition, triggers, desires, risks, guesses, and hopes. We take events personally that have little to do with us.

It can look like a big risk to stop raking ourselves over the coals. What if we really are not good enough? What if we suddenly lose all ambition to get things done? We fear that figuring out what is wrong with us is the only way to keep ourselves in line.

Perhaps you can give yourself permission to try kindness once and see what happens. You can always go back to the old way if the Inner Critic's predictions of disaster come true.

What is self-compassion? Even with permission to try self-compassion, it may not be obvious how to proceed. Perhaps giving yourself a hug or a pat on the arm feels good. Perhaps calling yourself "darling" or "dear" fills you with warmth. Or perhaps those actions feel fake, dangerous, painful.

Self-compassion can trigger emotional flashbacks in people who have been exposed to cyclical abuse where compassion was part of the setup for the next attack. It can also be difficult for those who grew up in emotionally neglectful homes and rarely received compassion.

Space for discovery. Take your time. Create space to discover true kindness, rather than pretending or assuming you know how kindness feels for you. Ask yourself what would feel good in this moment. What would you say to someone you love in similar circumstances? What would allow you to receive the same kindness? What have friends said or done in the past that eased your heart?

Compassion for not knowing. You could start by acknowledging that it is hard not to know what kindness feels like. Breathe in with all the others in the world who do not know. Stand with yourself quietly in not knowing.

Compassion for self-judgment. When you hear judgmental, angry, or scornful words in your head, you could acknowledge that it is hard to hear those words. Breathe in with all the others in the world judging ourselves right now. Hold both the accuser and the accused in your awareness, and notice that your containing awareness is larger than both of them.

Compassion for confusion. In painful situations where despite our best efforts we cannot figure out how we got there or how to get out, we can give ourselves compassion for confusion. "It's hard to be confused and not to know how to improve a situation. People get confused and stuck all the time. I want to stand with myself in this hard place."

Compassion for shame. Next time you feel cringing shame about something you did, notice your suffering. Gently, remind yourself that cringing shame and doing things wrong are part of being human, and that it is a hard place to be. Give yourself sympathy for the pain you experience. "Shame hurts. It's okay to make a mistake. Everyone does. You don't have to be perfect."

Permission. People often need a helping hand to make the leap from, "I can't possibly be good enough," to "I have always been good enough." Here is your Official Permission to believe you are good enough right now, yes, even you, with all your mistakes and successes and confusions and clarities. We have all always been good enough.

Heritage of Resilience

Traumas often repeat across generations, sometimes despite our best efforts to take a different path. When we find ourselves repeating a pattern, we can compassionately acknowledge our frustration and treat ourselves with kindness. Resilience also repeats across generations as survivors teach their strengths through stories and behavior.

Resilience is:

- Ability to recover from shock or injury.
- Inner recognition of support and warning of danger.
- Stubbornness to keep looking for a better way.
- Yielding and springing back into shape like a living tree branch.

What does resilience mean to you?

Explore your heritage. Does your heritage form part of your conscious identity, or do you think of yourself as "regular, plain"? In what ways are you alike and different from the people around you? When you meet someone, what qualities feel familiar and comforting (or threatening)? What qualities grab your attention with their unfamiliarity?

Are you surrounded by cousins and aunts, or do you stay as far as possible from your relatives? If you were adopted you may have put great effort into connecting with people who share your genetic heritage. We absorb patterns from both our genetic relatives and the family we interact with.

Persistent echoes. Unprocessed trauma echoes down generations. Present but unnamed, it exerts an increasing pressure on the people carrying it, bending their behavior around it. Children absorb these altered behavior patterns without understanding them, like a family that habitually walks around a hole in the porch even after it is repaired. We may feel confused and ashamed that we avoid that section of the porch "for no reason." We consciously understand that it has been repaired and "there is nothing to be afraid of," but the unresolved trauma pushes us to detour with surprising force.

Acknowledge behaviors. When we acknowledge our patterns of behavior and listen for the truths behind them, the behavior begins to shift without a battle. Someone who fell through the porch might need to gently remember the sensations and emotions involved. Someone who witnessed the fall has a different set of sensations and emotions to process.

Someone who grew up veering around that part of the porch because everyone else does will hear inside that the restriction has no internal foundation and cross the porch with a light heart. We might want to skip directly to the realization without listening first, but the awareness has to come from within.

Listen for underlying truths. Do you find yourself unhappily echoing family behaviors? What happens when you acknowledge that yes, you have behaved that way, and listen quietly for more information? You could try this to gain insight into family patterns even if you do not participate in them. In some small way, they may resonate inside you.

As we gradually clear out unresolved trauma, our

inherited resilience shines through, sometimes in the trauma responses themselves. Avoiding a hole in the porch is a survival skill. Awareness gives us a choice about when to use it.

Seek family stories. Family stories often contain traumatic events as an unspoken backdrop, matter-of-factly accepted as the way things are. Resilience weaves through the stories, including in how the stories are told or avoided. If you are in contact with them, you could ask family members for stories of surrenders in their lives. Listen for their strengths.

For example, my German-Jewish grandparents escaped genocide by fleeing their homes in the late 1930s and starting over in Santiago, Chile. In the mid-1960s the political situation in Chile looked dangerous, so my relatives relocated again, scattering across three continents. I inherited a complicated answer to "Where are you from?" and a wary readiness to pull up roots and start over when necessary.

Recognize resilience. We may take family strengths for granted because "everyone does that" or "that's easy." What qualities helped your people survive to bring you into the world? How do those resilient qualities manifest in you? Watch for the strengths you and the people around you use to get through each day.

Discover Your Core Commitments

One source of resilience is the commitments at our core. Our commitments are both privately entwined with our core values and publicly announced by our relationships and actions. The pledges we make to others and ourselves form a large part of our identity.

Even though we think of commitments as fixed, all but the deepest commitments can change in response to changing circumstances. Commitments vary in length, motivation, and depth of meaning.

Forced commitments are executed by willpower, with an implied battle between the part making the commitment and some other part that must be overcome. The commitment might be a "self-improvement" effort, or be demanded by someone else.

A forced commitment is likely to end when it incurs costs that affect other commitments, or when the resisting part gains ascendancy. Costs can include time, energy, or emotional disruption as well as money.

Some commitments are forced by a desire to avoid uncertainty or to bargain with the future. If we unconsciously expect a commitment to guarantee success, we can be painfully surprised by a negative outcome. There is a myth that commitment to a shaky relationship can fix it, as if doubt caused the shakiness rather than vice versa.

As you think of forced commitments you have made, compassionately notice the motivations behind them. What problems were you solving? What parts of yourself were you fighting?

Trial commitments are time-limited experiments to evaluate the costs and benefits of an action. They can be canceled in the case of unexpected complications.

Several years ago, I made a trial commitment to stop eating wheat for two weeks and evaluate whether it helped my symptoms of exhaustion and brain fog. I gathered some wheat-free foods in advance and gave myself permission to ease into the restriction.

Is there a trial commitment you could make to address a sensitivity or other issue in your life? Think about ways to make it easier and start gradually.

Ongoing commitments are open-ended, habitual, and continue because the benefits outweigh the costs. They can be re-evaluated and discontinued when circumstances change.

I saw an immediate improvement in my symptoms during the trial commitment, so I continue to avoid eating wheat. I could choose to eat a food with wheat if it were worth the consequences, but I prefer to feel energetic and clear-headed.

Careers, relationships, hobbies, and beliefs are all built from ongoing commitments. When commitments are woven into our self-image, change can be wrenching. I would be delighted to find that I can eat wheat again, and at the same time it would be a big change in how I relate to the world. When feeling stuck, one option is to re-evaluate ongoing commitments.

What are some of your ongoing commitments? Have you changed an ongoing commitment in the past? What situation might convince you to change one in the future?

Core commitments, often unspoken, guide our decisions about ongoing commitments. We have core commitments to survival, well-being, and nourishment, and against pain, loss, and abandonment. My core commitment to feeling well underlies my ongoing commitment to avoid eating wheat.

Like faith, core commitments are part of who we are, discovered rather than decided. What core commitments are supported by your current ongoing commitments? What do you need or long for no matter how hard you try to leave it behind? What do you reach toward no matter how many obstacles stand in your way?

Core commitments to connection, openness, and honesty can be used as hooks to control people. If you have been the victim of manipulation or emotional abuse, you might feel stupid, vulnerable, or ashamed when you think about your core commitments. Gently remind yourself that abuse reflects badly on the abuser, not on you. The intrinsic value of your self and your core commitments cannot be damaged by abuse.

External pressure. Abusers commonly pressure their targets for premature commitments, ensuring that the targets' sense of integrity holds them in the relationship as the abuse intensifies. Pressure for a quick commitment is a red flag for manipulation. Commitments come from within, and pressure is a boundary violation.

Salespeople sometimes use similar techniques to conflate a prospective customer's commitment to a goal with a commitment to the product or service being sold. "Prove your commitment to your health by buying this product!" The core commitment to health exists whether or not the customer chooses to make the purchase.

Never again. Survivors of abusive relationships often

vow, "Never again!" Do you carry any ongoing commitments against past events? Take some time to think or write about what, specifically, you do not want to repeat. Your list might be long, detailed, and full of strong feelings, or it might contain a single encompassing phrase. How does it feel in your body to acknowledge these commitments?

Into the unknown. A commitment against repeating the past can lead to commitments for new actions. An abuse survivor might commit to learning about healthy relationships and boundaries. Does your list imply any commitments for action? The first step is a commitment to sitting with the unknown, since your existing skills and knowledge were not enough to avoid the problem last time.

Forgiveness for past decisions. We all make ongoing commitments, even if only a commitment against being entrapped by commitments. We have all had commitments lead us in unexpected directions. Whether you have judged yourself for keeping a commitment or for leaving one behind, consider forgiving yourself for past decisions. When your identity is grounded in your core commitments, you can weather changes in ongoing commitments more easily.

Stand in Your Story

Josie wants to cut off contact with a family friend, ending an ongoing commitment to spend time with him. He sexually assaulted her long ago. Even though he has behaved courteously since then, she has never felt comfortable around him. She wrestles with how to tell her partner and son, preemptively arguing with expected objections. Her partner is usually supportive, but their fifteen-year-old son, like his grandparents, frames everything in terms of how it will affect him. Josie struggles with old defensive patterns with him.

Josie's parents were emotionally abusive. Rather than support and celebrate her individual self, they narcissistically expected her to echo their opinions. When she stood up for herself, they responded with cruelty and contempt. Josie learned to dissociate from her viewpoint in favor of the opponent's side in the name of being "objective."

Internalized opponents. We internalize opposing viewpoints in order to counter them, or to understand how to fit in. While that can be a useful survival skill, it diverts energy and momentum away from what we want to accomplish. Instead of advocating fully for ourselves, we divide our energy between ourselves and our internalized opponents.

Not so objective. Calm, rational, scientific statements are often considered superior to emotional personal opinions. People with power and privilege are more likely to be calm because they are not feeling threatened, and their opinions are more likely to be supported by the majority.

While it is respectful to consider others' viewpoints, it is not objective to abandon internal experience and intuition, even when many others disagree. Even a scientifically "objective" viewpoint is subject to the cultural biases of the scientists performing the experiments. When cis white heterosexual men are the default, seemingly objective results are tilted toward their experiences.

Not subject to a vote. It is healthy to value your own viewpoint, no matter how personal and emotional. No one will value it as much as you do. "Everyone else thinks..." is not a reason to change your story. Your perceptions are not subject to a vote.

Listen inside for your story. Josie pauses to separate the past from the present. She listens to the young part of her that believes she does not matter as much as the people around her. She listens to the part that always believes she matters, who has fought for her even when it would be more convenient to keep a low profile and escape notice. Her gut announces with certainty that she is done hanging out with Evan as if nothing happened. She remembers times her partner has responded well when she takes a stand. She realizes that her son will adapt and learn from her strength.

Josie speaks clearly from her truth, making space for others to speak without assuming what they will say. "I no longer want to see our friend Evan or invite him to our house. He hurt me a long time ago, and I've never felt comfortable around him. Let's talk about how this can work for all of us."

Centered and stable. When she stands in her own story, others can speak from their stories without knocking her off center. When her partner brings up Evan's feelings, she answers, "I've protected his feelings long enough. Now I'm protecting mine."

One of the responses Josie feared is, "But he's kind to me!" When she stands in her own story, she can recognize this as a separate story. "I'm glad he's kind to you. That doesn't change how I feel."

As she expected, her son brings up the passage of time and the redemption narrative. "It's been so long. Just let it go. Evan has changed." Josie responds, "I hear that you'd prefer this wasn't an issue. It still is for me. This is my story, not Evan's." As a family they discuss that forgiveness is a private process that cannot be forced. Without an apology and amends, forgiveness might include not wanting to see him.

Resolving her internal conflicts helped Josie give her family an opportunity to hear her. In addition, her family cares enough about her well-being to listen. The conversation had room for everyone's stories.

Unheard stories. If she had been speaking with narcissists, she might have heard, subtly or overtly, "How dare you say anything? You are so selfish, wanting something to be about you (instead of about us)." No amount of preparation can force others to listen with respect rather than bullying us into agreement.

Another common bullying technique is "You shouldn't feel that way," or the tone argument, "You're too emotional." Emotions are personal, private, and get to be how they are for as long as they are. Emotions remind us about our stories when we have suppressed them for so long we forgot they existed.

Confusion. When there is no room for our stories, we begin to wonder if we really are taking up too much space, or if we need to improve our communication skills, or if our story is valid at all. Abusers take advantage of this confusion and use gaslighting to cover for abuse.

- That doesn't hurt.
- You're imagining things.
- You had an orgasm so you wanted it.

A physiological reaction does not imply consent. Our body's experience belongs exclusively to our own story. It is a boundary violation for someone to claim they know more about it than we do. When someone overrides our story, we might feel angry, resentful, dissociated, or less connected. We might notice tightness and contraction, or a need to physically take up more space.

Each story is valid. Each viewpoint and story is valid, including those that are uncertain, unsure, or conflicted. We can take all the time we need to form our own conclusions. It can feel risky, even life-threatening, to take a stand in our story if it led to punishment in the past. When each person owns their story in a conversation, we can feel open, centered, stable, relieved. Where and how do you already stand in your story?

Connect with Your Complex Voice

When we free our voices, we can more easily express our stories. Too many of us believe we need to improve our voices in some way. Whether singing or speaking, we manipulate our voices to sound softer, stronger, clearer, calmer, or otherwise more "socially acceptable" than our unimpeded voices.

In addition to controlling how we sound, we carefully control what we say. Old threats, shame, and uncomfortable reactions keep us silent about traumas we have experienced. Many abused children grow up with an iron-clad rule to keep home and school separate and "act normal" to hide the abuse from outsiders.

Isolation after trauma. Survivors often extend the rule of silence into adulthood, maintaining a thick wall of shame between inner and outer experience. At the same time, desires for rescue and connection create an inner demand to speak, to tell, to be heard and understood. Behind the protective wall, survivors feel isolated and bereft, sentenced to separation from the rest of the human race.

Intellectually we may understand that humans both inflict and endure trauma every day in every environment, from bullying to assault to "unspeakable" rape and torture of children. Emotionally the sense of separation persists.

In part, that feeling is a longing for connection with ourselves. The overwhelming shock of trauma divides us from our bodies through dissociation and denial. Shocked out of wholeness, we lose the way back to ourselves and feel permanently exiled.

Social isolation can trigger stored feelings of catastrophic isolation and helplessness during trauma. It can help to remember that while isolation is uncomfortable in the present, it is no longer an immediate emergency. The present offers more tools to reach out, including the voice.

Release the effort. Like breathing into your back, you can free your voice by releasing effort rather than trying harder. In each of these simple steps, notice where the effort is. What muscles are tense? Is there a sense of pushing through or holding back?

1. Say a word out loud. "Hum."
2. Start to say it again, but don't. What stops the sound?
3. Say "Hummmmmmmmm," extending the "m." Now you're humming.
4. Start to hum again, but don't. What stops the sound? Is it different from what stops you from saying a word?
5. Start humming again. What shifted to allow the sound to emerge? Can you allow more of that?

Sometimes the whole body tackles the voice on its way out. If you cannot bring yourself to hum out loud, notice whether it is safe in the present to make noise. You could do the exercise mentally, or imagine humming to a small child. We instinctively connect to children with sound.

Add vibration. Try the following exercises to encourage your voice to vibrate in your bones and allow vibrations to extend outward from your body. When we tried these in a workshop, vibrations spread and pooled together and palpably connected us to each other.

- As you hum, sense for vibration from the inside in your belly, chest, throat, face. Do your lips tingle?
- Imagine your voice resonating in your spine, the column of bones rising through your center.
- Cup your jaw with a gentle curious hand. Can you feel vibration from the outside? Where you find vibration, keep humming into that place and let the vibration grow.
- Is it easier to find vibration at a higher pitch? How about a lower one?
- What do you notice when you relax your jaw down and forward with your mouth still closed? You might hear more overtones and harmonics.
- Notice how the sound changes as you move around. Tilt your head, move your shoulders, twist, lean forward. When the hum sounds louder and buzzier, allow more of that motion.

Complex, resonant. Make space for your voice to be complex, resonant, messy, vibrant, unbalanced, unconstrained. Make space for the constraints as well, those rules and tensions that have helped you navigate an uncertain world. Vibration touches the constraints and invites them to soften. Consider allowing your past to color your voice, neither hidden nor shouted, but part of what shaped you.

Notice how you respond to complex, resonant voices around you. Despite our internal rules about how we should sound, we are often drawn to open, authentic sound from others.

Hum to make contact. Next time you feel isolated or disconnected, try humming to connect with your body. Hum to your lonely child self still longing for rescue. Hum to the part that hurts, emotionally or physically. As you make contact, you may feel the abandonment or pain or stuckness more intensely at first. Let vibrations move through you, jostling stuck energy into healing motion.

Available for connection. The voice can be a tool for manipulation, tightly controlled to elicit the responses we want. It can also be a tool for expression to reflect the truth within. We can choose how much to let the truth show. As we release our voices to move through us and reach beyond us, we become more available for connection with ourselves and others.

Repair Your Reality After Gaslighting

In the movie *Gaslight*, Gregory sets out to convince his wife Paula that she is insane. He secretly removes items from their home and tells her she did it. He isolates her from others. He uses her growing distress to "prove" she is unstable. When she notices the gas lights in their home dim and flicker, he assures her she is imagining things.

The term gaslighting is now used to describe psychological abuse that attempts to destroy the victim's trust in their perceptions of reality. People who distrust their perceptions are easier to manipulate and control.

Abuse-related gaslighting. Not every instance of gaslighting is as blatant as hiding items or directly denying someone's perceptions. Most abuse includes an element of gaslighting. Abusers rarely say out loud, "I'm choosing to abuse you."

- A physically abusive spouse says, "I'm doing this for your own good. You shouldn't provoke me." In truth, victims do not cause abuse.

- A sexually abusive parent says, "This isn't happening. I love you. You like it. It doesn't hurt." In truth, abuse is not loving behavior. Children do not ask for assault. The pain is real.

- A ritually abusive group stages abuse so bizarre and extreme that victims do not believe their own memories. Real bloodshed and torture are combined with drugs and misdirection, adding to the sense of unreality.

Everyday gaslighting. Gaslighting occurs in more subtle ways as well, any time someone responds as if your reality does not exist.

- An adult says to a crying child, "There's no reason to be sad. Give us a nice smile."
- A partner says, "That's too hard for you. Let me do it."
- A friend snaps, "I'm not angry! Why are you starting a fight?"
- A narcissist reacts with so much contempt when you assert any needs that you feel like the selfish one.
- After being called on a racist or sexist comment, the speaker says, "Just kidding!" or "You're too sensitive!" or "You're looking for reasons to be offended."

Signs of gaslighting. Gaslighting can be hard to spot, especially when it has been happening for a while. When you have been taught to doubt your perceptions, it is difficult to assert that doubt is caused by something outside you. Suspect gaslighting when you notice:

- **Confusion.** You feel confused and off-balance when you interact with someone. You receive puzzling responses to ordinary actions, and your reactions are labeled wrong or unreasonable.
- **Fears about mental stability.** You worry that you are going crazy. Someone repeatedly expresses concern that you'll have a nervous breakdown.
- **Conflict about memory.** You hear, "I never said

that," when you clearly remember hearing it. You frequently hear, "You're imagining things," or "You remember that wrong." Memory differences can be expressed respectfully by saying, "I don't remember saying that," or "I don't remember it that way."

- **Emotional vertigo.** You have a sense of dizziness, or no place to stand, when you try to make sense of a situation. The facts do not add up, but you see that as a flaw in yourself rather than in the situation. This can lead to obsessive thoughts as you try to figure it out.

- **Distrust of your perceptions.** You ask others to confirm what you notice. When someone disagrees with you, you immediately assume you were wrong. Do you remember a time when you did trust your perceptions? When did that change?

Breathe into doubt. When you notice any of these signs, allow compassion for yourself. Breathe into your truth. "I don't know what to believe. I feel crazy." Bring kindness to your experience of confusion and doubt.

Keep a record. If you have enough privacy, it can bring relief to record your thoughts, feelings, and sensations. Your journal can receive your conflicting impressions without the need for certainty. If someone questions your memory, you can look back at your notes. If items mysteriously appear and disappear, you can take strategic photographs of problem areas.

Listen within. To rebuild self-trust and repair your reality, tune in to your internal signals with interested curiosity. In her book *The Power of Focusing*, Ann Weiser Cornell teaches Inner Relationship Focusing, a simple method for connecting with yourself. When you notice a sensation or emotion, you can keep it company, listening for its truth without expecting it to change.

- Something in me feels anxious, and I say hello to that.
- My belly feels tight, and I say hello to that.
- I don't know what I feel, and I say hello to that.

If you feel judgmental of what you notice, you can turn your listening attention toward judgment.

- Something in me hates that I feel anxious, and I say hello to that.
- Something in me wants my belly to relax, and I say hello to that.
- Something in me says I should know what I feel, and I say hello to that.

As you listen inside, your vague sensations will become more clear. As parts of you feel fully heard, they will shift and heal. As you practice listening, you will regain confidence in your perceptions.

Ignore motives. In the movie *Gaslight*, Gregory's manipulation of his wife is part of a hidden plot to find her aunt's jewels. Sometimes gaslighting helps an abuser maintain a more sympathetic self-image as well as concealing abuse. Gaslighting often lacks an apparent motive, which adds to the victim's confusion and self-doubt.

You do not have to figure out why someone is gaslighting you. You do not even have to label the behavior as gaslighting. You can simply say hello to your confusion and need to understand.

Seek out support. It can be tempting to ask others to

confirm your perceptions of gaslighting. Unfortunately, others may be unaware of what is happening and do not have your moment by moment observations. Turn your attention toward what is true for you.

- Something in me is uncertain, and I say hello to that.
- Something in me desperately wants confirmation, and I say hello to that.

Instead of taking a poll on whether your perceptions are correct, seek out people who support you in welcoming all your perceptions.

Rebuild self-trust. As you repair your relationship with yourself, the effects of gaslighting will gradually fall away. Over time, your boundaries will heal, and you will naturally say no to emotionally abusive behavior.

Trust Yourself Despite Everyday Gaslighting

Intentional gaslighting, the overtly abusive kind, can be more intense and severe, but everyday gaslighting is more insidious, permeating our social environment and sneaking inside our heads.

"I'd like a late afternoon appointment."

The dentist's receptionist responds, "How about 10am on Thursday."

"No, I'd like a late afternoon appointment."

"How about 1pm next Tuesday."

I say, sharply, "Did you hear me say *late afternoon?*"

"Oh, we save those for kids' orthodontic appointments, after school." If she had said that from the beginning instead of pretending not to hear my preference, I would not have felt shaken and angry at the end of the conversation.

Erased words, actions, perceptions. Everyday gaslighting, not acknowledging someone's words, actions, or perceptions, is distressingly common. Out of convenience or obliviousness, people respond based on their internal version of reality instead of what happens in the outside world. For the people on the other side of those interactions, it is crazy-making. "Maybe I forgot to say..." "Maybe I didn't really see..." "I wonder what I did wrong to make them respond that way..."

Reinforced doubt. Some children, usually boys, are

rewarded for being aggressive, certain, direct. They absorb that their opinions are important, respected, and probably correct. Other children, usually girls, are rewarded for being compliant, polite, yielding. They absorb that their opinions are unwelcome and probably wrong.

Partly because of those differing levels of internal doubt, we reflexively defer to those with more power and privilege, giving more weight to their version of events. In some conversations, for some topics, we are the ones with more power to assert reality.

Respond authentically. It takes time and care to respond authentically to what is in front of us instead of what we believe or wish to be true. To take responsibility for our mistakes and oversights. To be self-aware enough to choose our behaviors. To own our projections.

Within your areas of expertise and confidence, remember to make room for more tentative opinions. Take a moment to wonder what would have to be true to explain that person's experience. Take a moment to include the context of your expertise. "I see this all the time in my lab." "I read a recent blog post about that." "I have been biking around town for decades."

Condescending explanations. At the same time, you do not have to erase your expertise. Everyday gaslighting is a component of mansplaining, a term coined in response to Rebecca Solnit's elegant essay, "Men Explain Things To Me."* Mansplaining is when a man condescendingly explains to a woman something she already knows. He assumes he knows more and she knows less simply because of gender. He keeps talking even if she tries to interrupt to

---

* rebeccasolnit.net/essay/men-explain-things-to-me/

correct his assumption. His internal worldview is impervious to her experience and expertise.

Whitesplaining, straightsplaining, etc. are defined similarly. People with more power override the lived experience of people with less power, because they can. They ask wonderingly why people get so upset, because they are not the ones being erased.

Erased emotional labor. Everyday gaslighting occurs in relationships in many ways. For example, one person repeatedly ignores the clearly stated preferences of the other person. The oblivious person might never understand why the relationship ends, because the emotional labor of listening and remembering preferences is just not on their radar.

Harassment and bullying often have an element of everyday gaslighting. "Maybe he didn't mean to brush against me." "Maybe it's coincidental that I didn't get invited to that meeting." We try to think positive thoughts, give people the benefit of the doubt, and make room for the best outcome, ignoring the sick feeling in our gut that says, "That wasn't right."

We are told to simply doubt ourselves less, but people with less power who have the temerity to stand their ground assertively often get labeled "unhelpful," "bitchy," and "hard to work with."

Validating sentences. When a friend comes to you torn up inside because a situation does not make sense no matter how hard they try to figure it out, and they are sure something is wrong with them, and they feel like there is no solid ground under their feet, here are some validating sentences you can offer them.

- I believe you.
- You were right.

- That makes sense.
- It's not you.
- I see how hard you're working.
- You're doing all the right things.
- I trust your skills and your judgment.

How does it feel to imagine a kind friend saying those sentences to you?

Persistent confusion. When your distraught friend argues that they can see the other person's point, and maybe they are making a big deal out of nothing, and they should just be stronger and have a thicker skin, you can urge them to stand in their own story and give their emotions room to be there.

Persistent "unexplained" anger, confusion, and distress are warning signs for everyday gaslighting. Our emotions arise for good reasons, usually sparked by the present even when they are augmented from the past. When we allow all our emotions room to move, we gain valuable information about our own truth.

Shelter tentative truths. Protect faint and tentative truths inside. Shelter these new green shoots from the need for proof, either externally or internally. Let them be tentative, and nonetheless firmly there. "Everyone else says..." is not a relevant rebuttal to our lived experience. Neither is "You are too sensitive."

Responses in the moment. When you notice that someone is erasing your truth, you can always validate your truth inside, and talk to someone supportive later. As you evaluate your options, consider whether the person seems defensive or ashamed or dangerous. You could

- Let it go by without comment.
- Change the subject with small talk.
- Ask about their internal state.
- Name what they are doing: "You're implying that I'm crazy, or lying."
- Keep repeating your truth. "I'd like a late afternoon appointment."
- Show your anger or distress at being erased.

Whatever response you choose is the right response for that moment. Doubt and confusion are an intrinsic part of gaslighting. There is nothing wrong with how you feel, no wrong way to respond. The problem lies with them, not you. Consider extending yourself the benefit of the doubt.

Serenity Through Your Locus of Control

Grant me the serenity to accept the things I cannot change, the courage to change the things I can, and the wisdom to know the difference. — *Reinhold Niebuhr*

Locus of control is a psychological term for our beliefs about who controls the events in our lives. It can be internal (we have control) or external (outside forces have control). We can also be "bi-local" and believe in a mix of personal agency and external forces.

Internalized blame. At first, children do not differentiate between the outside world and their internal world. They naturally assume that there is an internal cause for everything that happens. Abusers often reinforce that belief. Referring to unwanted sexual touch, an abuser might say, "You asked for a hug, so you wanted this." Or, more directly, "You made me do this." A physical abuser might say, "You made me mad."

Children also internalize blame for abuse to avoid an intolerable double bind between the need to escape abuse and the need to trust caregiving adults. As painful as it is to believe they deserve abuse, it is less painful than believing that a caregiver chooses to hurt them.

External choice. Abuse also reinforces learned helplessness. "I tried my hardest to be good and the abuse is still happening, so I might as well not try." This might come from the realization that abusers make the choice to abuse, independent of the victim's behavior. Or, it might come from the mistaken belief that victims cause abuse, and some inherent flaw makes the abuse continue.

Reassign fault and power. One of the central tasks of healing is to reassign fault and power. Much less of the past was our fault, and at the same time we have more power in the present, than we believe.

Fluid categories. It sounds like the Serenity Prayer refers to rigid categories of what we can and cannot change, and wisdom lies in understanding them in advance. Instead, the Serenity Prayer refers to fluid categories that we discover in each moment. We gain wisdom about what we can and cannot change through experimentation. When an action works, then great! We can change that, this time. When an action does not work, we can practice serenity until we think of something else to try.

Brick walls and curtains. When we first confront a problem, we do not yet know if we face a brick wall, or a doorway covered by a curtain. As we attempt different solutions, we learn more about the problem. With an internal locus of control, the response to failure is to try harder and take failure personally. We imagine that we should be able to push through that brick wall.

With an external locus of control, the response is not to try at all and feel helpless. We forget to test whether we can push through a curtain.

With a bi-local approach, failure tells us that we are not the sole cause of the problem, and gives us more information about external causes. We can acknowledge a brick wall and continue to look for solutions.

For example, someone treats us unkindly. We can try to own our projections around unkindness. If that works, then the problem lay with us, and we fixed it. If it does not work, rather than trying harder, we can assume that the person is choosing to behave unkindly for their own reasons, which probably has nothing to do with us.

Other people are external to us. We can influence other people, or even command them, but ultimately other people's actions are not under our control. It can be a relief to drop the effort to control others and bring our attention back to choosing our own actions and beliefs.

Each of us is a part of larger systems: families, workplaces, communities, and whole societies. Our relative position of privilege or marginalization in each system is one of many external factors that affect the results of our actions. A cis white man encounters fewer obstacles than a trans Latina woman, simply because we unconsciously give cis white men the benefit of the doubt more often, and assist them more quickly. Systems tend to preserve the status quo.

At the same time, as a part of the system, anyone's actions might have unexpected leverage at a tipping point and cause change.

Separate fault and power. We may not have caused a problem, but we can try to find solutions. Absolving ourselves of fault can be a powerful first step to seeing a situation clearly. Asking, "What if this isn't my fault?" can lighten defensiveness and ease emotional pain. Energy that might have been spent on trying to fix ourselves can help find creative solutions instead.

Even if our action stops abuse, it does not make the abuse our fault. After years of abuse, a victim might set a clear boundary with an abuser one day. "I don't like that and I want you to stop." If the abuser stops, the abuse is still wholly the abuser's fault. If the abuser continues, the victim still successfully expressed a boundary.

The wisdom to explore the difference. In each situation, there is something we can change, if only to decline to blame ourselves for factors outside our control.

We do not need to determine in advance what is within our power to change. We do not need to have a fixed locus of control, whether internal or external. We can continue to explore the fluid boundaries between our power and our vulnerability, and practice serenity as we learn.

Resources

Self-Compassion: The Proven Power of Being Kind to Yourself, William Morrow, 2015, by Kristin Neff, Ph.D. contains many great ideas about self-compassion from her perspective as a professor of psychology.

Karla McLaren's *The Language of Emotions: What Your Feelings are Trying to Tell You,* Sounds True, 2010, contains deep understanding and practical tips about how emotions support us in our stories.

Ann Weiser Cornell's *The Power of Focusing: A Practical Guide To Emotional Self Healing,* New Harbinger Publications, 1996, is a clear, welcoming introduction to Focusing.

"On Gaslighting" by Nora Samaran advocates fierce compassion for the feeling of losing one's sanity. I highly recommend all of Nora Samaran's writing, including her essay on Nurturance Culture, which eloquently describes adult attachment.

norasamaran.com/2016/06/28/on-gaslighting/

norasamaran.com/2016/02/11/the-opposite-of-rape-culture-is-nurturance-culture-2/

Rebecca Solnit's classic essay "Men Explain Things To Me" lays out the silencing force of men's assumptions about women's incompetence.

rebeccasolnit.net/essay/men-explain-things-to-me/

6: Hard Times

Unfortunately, regaining self-trust in our perceptions and decisions does not make us immune to abuse and hard times in the present. No matter how hard we work to heal, we will continue to encounter individual abusive interactions and systemic injustice.

As we gain clarity about racism, sexism, ableism, homophobia, and all the other ways society is tipped to favor some people over others, we can both stand our ground against bullying and act with care when we have power.

We all need to be heard, acknowledged, and treated with respect. Present difficulties tangle with past trauma by setting off flashbacks, rubbing salt in unhealed wounds, and exposing missing resources and support. When we can hold onto self-trust, it helps steady us through those challenges.

When we feel stuck, helpless, or inadequate to the core, we can say hello to our experience, treat ourselves with kindness, and reach out for support.

Truth Across Lines of Authority

Monique deflected the young white woman's hand away from her afro and rolled her eyes. She was here to enjoy the party with her friends, not be treated like an exotic object. Just yesterday she stood uncomfortably still while her older white male coworker patted her head in passing.

Have you had the experience of responding two different ways to the same clear boundary violation? Afterward, you may have berated yourself for one or both responses, or you may have known exactly what calculations went into your decision.

At the party, Monique trusts her friends' knowledge of issues around touching Black people's hair. At her job, there are few Black women. Most people there would see themselves in her coworker's position by default, causing them to sympathize with him rather than supporting her boundaries.

Power calculations. Boundaries form a flexible container for our sensations, emotions, and preferences. We often think of boundaries as fence lines around what we control, markers for our sphere of authority. We should at minimum have sole authority over our own bodies. Where everyone is respectful, we express boundaries freely. Where those with more power transgress against those with less, we perform complex calculations about hierarchies of authority before we speak.

Even when we strive to treat everyone equally, it is easier

to express a boundary to people who have less power than we do. Not only is there less risk of retribution, but they are more likely to watch for our non-verbal signals of discomfort.

People with more power may subtly inhibit us from expressing boundaries. They may ignore non-verbal signals, loom just a little, or mention past violence. In interactions where you did not express a violated boundary, what influenced your decision not to speak?

The system is skewed. In addition to hierarchies based on age and authority, we live in a web of hierarchies based on privilege and marginalization. Characteristics such as skin color, gender, sexual orientation, religion, and level of health and ability all intersect to determine how much power we have in relation to others.

Privilege is like biking with a personal tailwind. Marginalization is like biking with a personal headwind. People with privilege get better results for the same amount of effort, and people who are marginalized have to work harder to keep up. White, male, cis-gendered, straight, Christian, able-bodied people are given preference in many subtle and overt ways. For example, men are hired more quickly than women* and white people are hired more quickly than Black people**.

Since headwinds and tailwinds are invisible, in any

---

* "How I Discovered Gender Discrimination"
whatwouldkingleonidasdo.tumblr.com/post/54989171152/how-i-discovered-gender-discrimination

** "Unemployed Black Woman Pretends to Be White, Job Offers Suddenly Skyrocket" by Yolanda Spivey
thewestsidegazette.com/unemployed-black-woman-pretends-to-be-white-job-offers-suddenly-skyrocket/

individual case it is easy to blame the person or the circumstances. In the aggregate, it becomes obvious that the system is skewed.

PTSD is an invisible disability. People who have experienced trauma are marginalized relative to people who do not have to contend with flashbacks, victim-blaming, and encounters with their abusers.

People with PTSD also have privilege relative to many people. Jaclyn, the young white woman who tried to touch Monique's hair, burst into tears when Monique blocked her hand. Jaclyn suddenly felt like she was facing her mother, who often hit her for mistakes. While Jaclyn fully deserves support and comfort for her distress, it is not Monique's responsibility to provide it.

Jaclyn could briefly apologize to Monique and seek comfort elsewhere. "I'm sorry. I shouldn't have tried to touch your hair."

Our place in the web. Most of us have a mix of characteristics that are privileged and marginalized. We may not notice the privilege that comes with characteristics seen as the default, such as being white, heterosexual, or able-bodied. What is your personal list of identities?

Next time you notice a boundary violation, take note of the lines of authority in the situation. Who has more privilege? Are there barriers to expressing the boundary? Does anyone show anger? People with privilege are free to express anger, while marginalized people are chastised for appearing angry even when speaking calmly.

In situations where you have less privilege, can you find a way to speak? Look for allies, and for power you do have to take action. Say a gentle hello to any feelings of helplessness that arise. Sometimes there is room to speak your truth, even when there is no room to enforce a boundary. "I don't like having my hair touched."

In situations where you have more privilege, can you make it safer for people to express boundaries to you? Stay aware of dominating body language, interruptions, and expecting others to yield to you. Speak less and listen more. Say a gentle hello to any feelings of defensiveness that arise.

Share power. It is distressing to have boundaries violated and feel unsafe to speak up. It is also distressing to be called out on a transgression or realize we have inadvertently contributed to oppression. Most of us find ourselves in both situations at different times, doing our best to bring awareness to lines of authority as we share power with those around us. Have compassion for your choices and the complex calculations beneath them.

Deflect the Tone Argument

Shantel examined the smartphone cases, debating which one to buy. A salesperson approached her. "Ma'am, I need to inspect your bag."

"That's racist! You're not inspecting white customers' bags!"

"They aren't mouthing off! Leave the store or I'll call security."

Tool for oppression. The salesperson used the Tone Argument to shift attention from his racist behavior to the tone of Shantel's statement. He used his power and position to silence Shantel and deny her access to the store's merchandise.

The Tone Argument is a specialized double bind used to silence people with less power or privilege.

- An angry tone is labeled "too aggressive" to hear.
- A quiet tone is labeled "too passive," easy to ignore or talk over.
- Naming the contradiction diverts attention from the original topic.
- Leaving ends the attempt to speak.

Avoiding discomfort. People with power and privilege take control to avoid sources of discomfort. Criticism of tone is backed up with power to set the terms of discussion. Variations of the tone argument include claims that a statement is not academic, erudite, fluent, or articulate enough to be valid. The reverse tone argument praises one statement for being calm and measured, criticizing others by implication.

Unequal responses. In the United States, Black people are stereotyped as angry, perceived as angry more quickly and penalized for it. The same statement about racism in the same tone from a white person would not evoke the same silencing reaction.

Similarly, women are stereotyped as emotional, perceived as emotional more quickly, and penalized for it. The same statement about sexism in the same tone from a man would not evoke the same silencing reaction.

In general, people with less power are seen as making trouble when expressing truths, boundaries, needs, desires, or other inconveniences for people with more power. While people with more power can be taken to task for their tone, it does not have the same systemic silencing effect.

No tone calm enough. A first-time recipient of the tone argument often takes it in good faith and tries hard to find the "right" tone. With repeated exposure it becomes clear that there is no tone calm enough to express uncomfortable truths to someone with the power to refuse to hear.

When someone uses the tone argument against us, we can first take a moment to internally validate the frustrating double bind and power dynamics of the situation. It is unfair to need to manage this person's power to silence our truth.

Then, we can evaluate the situation to decide which branch of the double bind to take. Our options include:

- Like Shantel, choose to speak angrily, or find anger spilling out. Anger carries power and emphasis.

- Choose to speak quietly and calmly. Perhaps they are ready to listen this time.
- Name the double bind: "Is there a tone that you would accept and hear my words?" "Can you reflect my message back to me even though you don't like my tone?"
- Choose to leave the situation or drop the attempt to speak, in fear for our safety or lacking the energy for this battle at this time.

Anger is a primal response to threat, invasion, and harm. When fight-or-flight reactions are interrupted during trauma, anger joins fear as part of PTSD. Anger is a valid, healthy reaction to past and present invasions.

Reactions to anger. While the truth and importance of a statement are independent of its delivery, many people find it difficult to listen to angry statements. It is our responsibility to manage our reactions to anger, especially when we have more power or privilege than the speaker. We can take a moment to check in with ourselves and honor our reaction without invalidating people's right to speak.

Many of us grow up in situations where anger was an excuse for violence. We might react to the presence of anger as an immediate emergency without realizing why. We can gradually learn to see anger with fresh eyes in structured situations, such as group therapy, where a facilitator holds safe space for both anger and fear of anger. Anger is not an attack in itself.

Respectfully hold space. Next time you are in the presence of an angry person, check with your intuition about whether they might become violent. If yes, take appropriate action to distance and defend yourself. If not, there is no immediate action you need to take.

The Tone Argument is used to bully people into silence. Rather than defend against anger, we can witness it and hold space for its expression, for ourselves as well as for others. It might feel like standing in a strong wind. The more space we create for anger, the more we respect each person's truths, boundaries, needs, and desires.

Interrupt Bullying

Bullying is **repeated, aggressive acts** in the context of a **power imbalance.** When we can name bullying, interrupt it, and hold perpetrators responsible for their behaviors, we can reduce pain and create a kinder environment for everyone.

Repeated. If we can stop a source of pain without other losses, the problem stops. A single hurtful act may be assault or abuse, but it does not become bullying until it is repeated.

Bullying includes a wrenching double bind.

- Bullying causes pain.
- Resisting bullying also causes pain.
- Naming bullying is strongly discouraged.
- Leaving can be impossible or costly.

Acknowledge the trap. Feeling powerless and trapped intensifies the pain of bullying. Acknowledging the double bind can lessen the sense of personal failure, since the situation is stacked against you. When there is no way to succeed outright, you can choose actions that work best for you.

Aggressive acts. Just as most sexual assaults are more subtle than being attacked in a dark alley, most bullying is more subtle than being knocked down for your lunch money. Bullying continues outside the schoolyard anywhere it is condoned, which is almost everywhere. Aggressive acts include physical and emotional attacks, manipulation, casual cruelty, and shows of force.

Isolation, exclusion, and withholding resources are also aggressive acts. Omissions can be hard to describe, making them terribly amenable to gaslighting ("What did they actually do to hurt you?") and self-blame ("Why don't they like me?").

Name bullying. When we name exclusion and other acts of omission as bullying, we hold the perpetrator and power structure responsible, rather than blaming the victim. Exclusion is still painful, but we can avoid agonizing obsessive attempts to fix ourselves in order to improve the perpetrator's behavior. Change in a victim cannot fix a perpetrator's problem.

Exploiting someone's vulnerability is also bullying. Teasing often does this under the guise of playfulness. If it hurts, it is an aggressive act. Victims often resolve to be tougher and less reactive. We all have vulnerabilities, and we deserve to be treated with kindness around them.

Power imbalances allow bullying to continue. A victim who has as much power as a bully could effectively say, "Stop that!" Bullying behavior may have an immediate goal of preventing or forcing some action, and/or a more general goal of intimidation and reinforcement of power imbalances.

Examine power structures. If you are being bullied, examine the power structures of the situation. List the ways the bully has more power, including social privilege, patterns and habits in your relationship, willingness to be more violent, or resources that the bully controls.

List the power you have in the situation. Claim the power to name your experience for yourself. You can also seek support and name your experience to others. Is there any power you can claim in relation to the bully? Perhaps the bully is a white male, but you are twenty years older and can claim the privilege and power of age.

If you said, "Stop that!" what would happen? Some bullies are cowards who back down in the face of resistance. Some become more aggressive. You are the best authority on the possibilities in your situation.

Interrupt bullying. Witnesses to bullying support power structures by doing nothing. As a bystander, if you say nothing, both the bully and victim think you support the bully.

As a bystander, examine the power you have. You can interrupt in the moment, confront the bully later, and/or support the victim later.

- Would you treat me that way?
- That's not cool.
- That's racist. That's sexist. That's homophobic. That's ableist.
- Wow.
- I saw that. I heard that.
- (To the victim) It's not your fault.
- (To the bully, assuming good intentions) Let's find a better way to express yourself.

Bystanders can avoid drama triangles by seeing each participant as a whole person rather than a caricature of a role. Look for the victim's power, the bully's compassion, and the bystander's needs. What goals does everyone have in common? These might include general goals of safety and happiness, or more specific goals such as enjoying a pleasant and successful work environment.

Like victims, bystanders can be shocked into silence by a bully's verbal violence. Bystanders may feel supportive but not know how to express it. Victims can request specific assistance during or after an incident.

- Did you see that?
- Thank you for being a witness.
- Let's talk about how to stop the bad behavior together.

Self-bullying. Bullying is endemic. Power imbalances permeate our society, beginning with the power imbalance between adults and children. Many people use aggressive acts to meet their goals.

We absorb these patterns of behavior and bully ourselves in an attempt to avoid external bullying. Our Inner Critics yell in the mistaken belief that we "should" become invulnerable. Unhelpfully, Inner Critics say, "Ignore them. You must be imagining it. It's something you did wrong. You should be able to fix it."

When you notice internal bullying, you can interrupt by asking the Inner Critic, "What are you not wanting to happen?" Responses might include humiliation, rejection, standing out, or feeling powerless. As you listen, the Inner Critic can explore less painful strategies to reach these goals.

Aim for kindness. When you notice bullying and remember that bullies are responsible for their behavior, you are already disrupting abusive power imbalances. Expect kindness from yourself and others, and clearly recognize its lack. Delight in the company of people who aim for kindness with you.

Decipher the Silent Treatment

The silent treatment is a deeply painful form of bullying. **Three-year-old Malaika** walks determinedly through the crowd. "Daddy? Daddy? Daddy?" One of her dads spots her and scoops her up with great relief. Safe in his arms, she wails her distress at losing sight of them. He holds her close until she calms and wriggles to be put down. She runs around happily, secure in the knowledge that separation is soon followed by reunion.

Silence as abandonment. For infants, separation from caregivers is an immediate, life-threatening emergency. In a good-enough environment, babies learn to manage the nervous system stress of apparent abandonment through small separations and reunions. Young children explore and return to home base in a reassuring rhythm.

In abusive or neglectful environments, children learn that abandonment can happen at any moment and last for an unpredictable length of time. Their nervous systems remain on guard rather than returning to alert calmness.

When children need help, attention, or care, then silence becomes punishment. Their caregivers' unresponsiveness becomes a judgment on their value in the world. They try desperately to be "good enough" to deserve care, rather than understanding that all children deserve care and attention simply for existing.

Qualities of silence. Silence between two people can be warm, inviting, and peaceful, or cold, forbidding, and hostile. Non-verbal cues and the joint and separate histories of the two people shape how silence is interpreted.

The silent treatment is intentional shunning to show displeasure. It is outright abuse when directed at a child, and rarely justified when directed at an adult. The silent treatment can be a tool for manipulation, or it can be an expression of fear and anger at someone who cannot be avoided.

Silence leaves us wondering about its reasons. Is the other person angry? Did we commit some offense? Are they busy? Struggling with their own issues?

Filling gaps. When we lack full information about a situation, we unconsciously fill the gaps with our past experiences. As Malaika grows up, when someone ignores her or gives her the cold shoulder, her experiences give her the resilience to assume the behavior is unintentional, undeserved, and time-limited.

In contrast, someone with early experiences of abandonment and abuse will assume that silence is intentional, deserved, and permanent. The uncomfortable experience of being ignored in the present can trigger emotional flashbacks to the intense pain of being abandoned as a child.

Emotional flashbacks can be difficult to identify, since the emotions are re-experienced in the present. They are marked by

- Intense reactions to seemingly minor events
- Feeling like they will last forever
- Feeling physically small and helpless like a child.

Any emotion we experience is a valid, real reaction. It is not helpful or comforting to accuse ourselves of overreacting. If an emotion seems intense, endless, and overwhelming, we can ask inside if it is connected with the past. We can offer ourselves compassion for how much it hurts now, and how much it would hurt to feel like that as a child.

Responses to non-response. In the face of non-response, whether in person or to a message, we can

- Notice our first assumptions about the reasons for the silence
- Acknowledge that we do not have full information about the situation
- Acknowledge our responses to subtle non-verbal cues
- Choose to inquire, wait, or write off the interaction

Most positive reason. To help guide the choice, imagine the most positive reason for the silence. Perhaps the person is busy, or a message got lost, or they are thinking it over, or they believe no response is needed. In that positive scenario, does it make sense to reach out? In some cases, even the most positive scenario does not give enough reason to continue communicating with someone.

If we choose to inquire and receive a reassuring response, that may resolve the problem completely, or it may take time to fully repair the relationship. If the problem arises repeatedly, there may be differing rhythms of communication, or the person might be sending mixed messages about wanting to be in contact.

Waiting for a response can trigger anxiety and flashbacks after a childhood spent waiting to get away, to find safety. Without the rhythm of separation and reunion, there is no embodied experience of a wait being over.

Self-disclosure. Silence can be especially painful in response to vulnerable self-disclosure. The absence of a reassuring response can feel like judgment. We imagine the person might be thinking, "If you can't say anything nice, don't say anything at all." Checking in with them risks a withering blast of contempt.

The person's silence lets us hear the Inner Critic's voice, and feel the part that believes its messages. In this difficult situation, bring in compassion. We can let the Inner Critic know that we hear its worry. We can let the believing part know that we hear its pain.

In dialogue with old pain. We are all in dialogue with old pain, including the person who is not responding. Their silence might come from fear, distraction, or dissociation. Silence might be their only available tool to disengage from a dynamic that is toxic *for them* (which is not a judgment on us).

Soften silence. Sometimes we are the ones not responding, out of busyness, inattention, reading email hurriedly on our phones, or the need to create distance. We can acknowledge vulnerable messages quickly with an estimate of when we can respond more fully. In most situations, if we need more distance, we can kindly say so without further excuses or explanations. Our experiences with someone let us know when silent withdrawal is the safest course of action.

We can guide others by requesting an acknowledgment and response time for important messages. We can protect ourselves by exposing a small amount of vulnerability at a time.

If we find ourselves giving someone the silent treatment, we can search for alternatives, such as avoiding them entirely, keeping interactions brief and formal, or letting them know we need a break from interacting with them. We can seek out mediation and community support. We can take note of community structures that lack support for fractured relationships, especially those fractured by abuse.

Sitting with silence. Silence is ambiguous, mysterious, changeable, and powerful. Notice how you fill silent gaps. Do you take them in stride, like Malaika, or assume you are somehow at fault? When do you fall silent? How have you resolved painful silences in the past?

The Betrayal of Not Being Heard

Society tells us in a lot of subtle and overt ways not to talk about abuse. It is uncomfortable to hear. There is no easy response. It challenges the dominant narrative that abuse only happens far away, to "them", not "us."

Need to be heard. At the same time, there is internal pressure to talk about our abuse history. We want to share important truths rather than hide behind a bland facade. We want to be visible. We need validation, acknowledgment, and support. We hope friends or professionals will come through, listening sympathetically, speaking kindly, and holding space for our stories.

Clear distress signals. There is an additional pressure to be heard after abuse: the burning memory of not being heard during abuse. People give clear distress signals when something hurts or is unwanted. An abuser intentionally overrides those signals or blocks them out. After abuse, something inside says, "Hear me. Tell me I didn't deserve that." Something else says, "I have to keep it a secret because maybe I did deserve that."

When the abuser is a parent, partner, or other trusted figure in our lives, we experience their ignoring our distress as a fundamental betrayal from someone who should protect us. We try to be louder and clearer, desperate to be understood. We wonder why this person believes that we deserve abuse. We begin to believe that there is something intrinsically wrong with us.

Not our fault. People "helpfully" tell us that the problem is our communication skills, or our boundaries, or our choice of parents, or our passivity, or our assertiveness. We twist ourselves into knots trying to fix ourselves, when the problem is not in us at all.

In truth, no one deserves abuse for any reason. We all deserve to have our distress heard and heeded.

Stay aware. We all make mistakes and cause pain. We get wrapped up in our own concerns and goals, and forget to be mindful of the people around us. We go on autopilot, or dissociate, or get overwhelmed by emotion. When we realize we hurt someone, we can apologize and reaffirm our commitment to stay aware.

Power dynamics. Those mistakes are different from systematically believing that others are unimportant, or denying that our actions will cause pain. We are socialized to listen carefully to people with more power and privilege, and disregard those with less.

When someone with less power becomes loud, angry, or demanding about not being heard, we invoke the Tone Argument and say we would listen if only they were more quiet and polite. We demand the same impossible tight-rope walk from ourselves, trying to find a polite way to be heard by people with more power.

Action steps. How can we productively handle a situation where our distress is not being heard?

Start with self-care:

- **Acknowledge** to yourself, "I am not being heard." This may be a painful pattern in your life.
- Remind yourself that it is **not your fault**. You

deserve to be heard.

- **Find allies** who hear you with caring. Ask for support.
- **Listen inside.** Hear your truth, even if no one else will hear you. Listen for what your Inner Critic is afraid of, and listen for the voices underneath that.
- **Notice the quality** of your inner listening. If we were parented brusquely, impatiently, resentfully, we tend to parent ourselves the same way. Seek out models for kind, compassionate listening.
- **Anchor in the present.** Take an inventory of your adult skills and choices. Check whether feelings of being powerless or trapped are partly flashbacks to past trauma.

Sadly, there is no single tool to open the ears and heart of someone who is not listening. Some people might need a brief reminder, while others are unreachable. Here are some strategies to consider.

- Most people react defensively to being told directly they are not listening. **"I don't feel heard"** might work better.
- A **question in a neutral tone** might get through. For example, "Do you believe you are hearing what I said?" or "Is there something in the way of hearing me?" or "What would help you hear me better?"
- You could try **modeling good listening** in hopes that the person will feel heard and then be able to reciprocate.

- **Stating concrete needs** might help. "I need you to stop interrupting me." "I need you to repeat back what I just said." "It's really important to me that you hear this."
- You could ask a **more powerful ally** to support your message. Imagine how this would feel, even if you do not have someone to ask. You could bring in a more powerful voice yourself. "How would you respond if [more powerful person] said what I just said?"
- **Being vulnerable** is an option. "This really hurts!" You deserve to be heard whether you show vulnerability or not. You should not need to get upset or emotional before someone will listen.
- **Showing anger** is also an option. "Listen up!" You should not need to yell before someone will listen, either.
- Make **natural consequences** clear. "When you don't hear my distress, I don't want to be around you."
- **Walk away**. Take a break. Ask the person to think it over.
- Consider ways to **get your needs met** that do not require this person to hear you. Find the smallest set of statements you need to get across, and focus on those.

Your needs matter. Not being heard can be exhausting and triggering. It erodes trust. It generates a gaslighting effect where the person is so oblivious to our reality that we doubt ourselves. "Maybe I'm asking for too much. Why should my needs be a priority, anyway?" When caring is mixed with unwillingness to hear, it creates painfully confusing mixed messages.

Relief at being heard. It can be a huge relief to spend time with people who matter-of-factly listen to your words and take your well-being into account. How does it feel in your body when you remember or imagine being heard? Seek that out, and celebrate when it happens.

We can lavish that same care on ourselves, paying careful attention to our needs throughout the day. The old pain of being treated as if we were unimportant heals little by little when we spend time in environments where everyone's well-being is a priority.

Stuck in a Labyrinth

Being stuck can feel like being cornered with nowhere else to run, or struggling under a heavy weight, or sitting at the bottom of an empty well looking up at an impossibly distant light. What is your experience of being stuck?

You are not alone. Being stuck could be emotionally neutral. "I don't know what to do about that, and I'll wait until I do." More often, being stuck comes with intense, difficult emotions. We feel terrified, frustrated, exhausted, defeated, trapped. We judge ourselves for not knowing how to extricate ourselves immediately.

Give yourself permission to be exactly where you are. You are not alone in feeling stuck.

Elements of feeling stuck. Feeling stuck can arise from a mixture of internal and external sources from both the past and the present. Your responses are valid no matter what their source, and it can help to sort out the different elements.

- **Flashbacks.** Traumatic events almost always involve some aspect of being unable to get away. Feeling stuck in the present can trigger memories of past trauma, with all the associated emotional intensity. Is there any part of being stuck in the present that has familiar echoes from the past, or feels like it will last forever?

- **Sensitivities.** When you are sensitive to certain foods or chemicals, accidental exposure can lead to brain fog, depression, and feeling overwhelmed. Do you feel more stuck at some times than others while your circumstances are unchanged?

- **Double binds.** Double binds lead to feeling stuck when you are pinned between contradictory demands. When you name the elements of a double bind, it clarifies that you are not to blame and helps you evaluate your options.
- **Recurring patterns.** A recurring pattern can leave you feeling stuck when you observe yourself moving through the pattern, unable to change it. Ironically, you feel most stuck as the pattern begins to shift, since your observation is already a change.
- **Spiritual losses.** There may be a spiritual losses involved. Perhaps you have faithfully made sacrifices and tried your best, and now feel betrayed by the results. You might notice grief, anger, disappointment, or bitterness as you sit with feeling stuck.

Say hello to your truth and judgments. When you feel stuck, acknowledge your reality. "Something in me feels stuck. I say hello to that." Say hello to any emotions, images, and physical sensations that emerge.

Also say hello to any judgments that arise. Perhaps something in you thinks you should try harder, figure it out faster, think more positive thoughts, feel sweeter emotions, or otherwise have a different experience than feeling stuck right now. "Something in me wants this to be different. I say hello to that."

A labyrinth, not a maze. Being stuck can feel like being lost in a maze, choosing turns at random, unintentionally going in circles, stopping in despair. Unlike a maze, a labyrinth has only one path through it, twisting and doubling back on itself, but always making forward progress.

You can use your finger or a pointer on a small labyrinth like the one on the next page, or find a nearby labyrinth* to walk. As you move mindfully along the single path into the center and then out again, make room for your actual experience, rather than what you think you should be experiencing.

What is it like for you to approach the center, only to swing around it into yet another set of zig-zags? What do you notice when the center finally opens before you? Do you follow the labyrinthine path outward, or simply leave?

As you move through the labyrinth, you might notice blissful peace, or bored impatience, or some mixture of both. You might feel most engaged while moving inward, or pausing at the center, or moving outward. Does any part of your labyrinth traversal feel like an achievement or relief?

Turn away. Sometimes there is no direct path to a goal, and turning away can help you move forward in unexpected ways. Indulge in distractions, get some sleep, and let the back of your mind work on the problem. Turn your attention toward what works well in your life. What challenges have you overcome in the past? If nothing comes to mind, carry those questions around with you and invite answers to arise.

Perhaps you can make progress in an area unrelated to the stuck problem. You could sweep the floor or pull weeds

---

* labyrinthlocator.com/locate-a-labyrinth

in the garden or make some other small satisfying change in your environment.

Wait and rest with kindness. Even when we feel the most stuck and helpless, time is still moving forward. The world is changing in tiny and large ways, and we change with it. When we run out of ideas, or energy, or hope, we can allow ourselves to wait and rest with as much kindness as possible.

Chartres Labyrinth. "Walk" with your finger or a pencil.

Surrender Without Shame

Remembered feelings of helplessness, vulnerability, and submission can be some of the most painful parts of healing from abuse. We are taught to believe that defeat, failure, and weakness are causes for shame. Instead, perpetrating abuse is the shameful act.

Surrender is a crucial survival tool. Like the physical freeze response, psychological surrender is our best attempt to reduce our suffering in an uneven battle. Your painfully remembered surrender was a successful strategy to survive into this present moment.

Failure is universal. Defeat and failure are universal experiences as we take risks, learn new skills, and venture into the unknown. We may feel terribly alone when we feel blocked, trapped or stuck, but those feelings are part of life around the world, throughout time.

Weakness is relative. As children, we are weaker than the adults around us. As adults in a hierarchical world, we might have less power than:

- Men who cat-call our womanly figures on the street
- White restaurant hosts who turn away from our brown faces
- Teammates who taunt us for "acting gay"
- Anyone who provides a survival need, such as a paycheck or a place to live.

In each interaction, we choose among many options,

including to speak up, to avoid conflict, or to surrender. It is not shameful to be weaker than some and stronger than others. Self-care includes giving ourselves room to be vulnerable, to lack the energy to fight, and to choose actions that preserve our safety, including compliance.

Waiting is an action. During a short-term assault or long-term abusive situation, waiting for an opportunity to escape is an important, undervalued survival skill. Waiting is a temporary surrender while gathering information and resources for future movement.

Healing after surrender. Surrender can be emotionally expensive, damaging our pride, dignity, and self-esteem. Surrender often involves forced compliance with boundary violations, leaving behind not only injured boundaries, but also misplaced shame for giving in.

To heal from surrender, take some time to say hello to the painful feelings that surround its memory. Create a space for them to speak, and keep them company with compassion. As you listen over time, the wider story around the need for surrender emerges, opening the way for self-forgiveness.

Learned helplessness. When we are forced to surrender too many times or for too long, we absorb the lesson that we are always helpless. We surrender our hope that someday we will escape, grow, change, and heal. Even when the external trap is gone, the internal limits remain in place.

Notice success. One solution for learned helplessness is to pay attention to your effective actions in the present. Absorb each success, no matter how tiny, and allow it to gradually counteract the old lesson of helplessness. Give yourself credit for the daily maintenance of living. Instead of looking beyond success to your failing edge, look beyond failure to your successful core skills. Imagine your three-year-old self watching your adult abilities with awe.

Remember hope. Another solution for learned helplessness is to reach into the past before the events that caused surrender. Perhaps your three-year-old self carries buoyancy, hope, and confidence that your adult self has lost. Look inside for a spark of faith in your power to survive and create change.

Surrender into healing. Instead of humiliation, some surrenders bring relief and forward motion. Tightly-held muscles finally surrender into support. A shield of denial is surrendered into deeper contact with our truth. Surrender to a long-fought obstacle allows movement in a new direction. These inner surrenders happen when the time is right, and cannot be forced.

Proud surrender. Can you find relief in past surrenders, or pride in your survival? Where in your life have you chosen to wait while you gather information and resources? When you consider surrender as a valid option, do you see a current situation in a new light?

The Puzzle Box of Shame

Sometimes, surrender and feeling stuck are part of a painfully slow deep healing process. We stop doing what does not work, and wait to find a new way that works better.

We are born needing physical and emotional contact to thrive. In addition to food and shelter, we need soothing touch and attuned mirroring to develop an emotionally stable self. We learn to trust our place in the world when we are welcomed with delight.

If the adults around us do not provide soothing touch and welcoming delight, we learn instead that we have to earn our place in the world by being quiet enough, or strong enough, or unemotional enough. We believe, before we have words, that there is something terribly wrong with us. We question our right to exist. We feel ashamed to the core.

An interpersonal problem. In her book *Understanding and Treating Chronic Shame*, Patricia A. DeYoung disagrees that shame is an individual problem. She defines shame as an interpersonal problem: an experience of one's felt sense of self disintegrating in relation to a dysregulating other. The dysregulation can come from overt emotional, physical, or sexual violence. Or it can be more subtle, someone turning away from our needs and emotions instead of turning toward us at crucial moments.

When someone notices our moments of disintegration and repairs the connection, we learn that shame is repairable. We implicitly learn the difference between guilt ("I did something bad") and shame ("I am bad"). We learn about remorse, apologies, and amends in response to guilt.

Dissociated disintegration. When there is no repair, we are left alone with unbearably painful disintegration. We flinch away from it with a sense of worthlessness, contempt, or disgust, and then dissociate from that. We reflexively veer away from further disintegrating encounters by making wordless rules.

- Don't reach out to that person when they're drunk.
- Don't reach out to that person.
- Don't reach out.

With our relational circuits shut down, we stumble through interactions with the people around us. We cope with isolation and ongoing pain through perfectionism, addictions, and the very best self-care we can manage.

Include the shamed self. We cannot reason our way out of chronic shame by dutifully repeating affirmations or deciding we should be over it. We imagine that healing means leaving behind our flawed, shamed self and building a new, whole, acceptable self. To truly feel better, we have to bring the shamed self with us.

Small shifts. Shame heals in small shifts, like one of those Japanese puzzle boxes that require many small moves on different sides before the lid finally slides open. Each time we encounter someone who offers warm, attuned emotional presence, the small wordless shamed part of us pays attention. We take tiny risks to reach out and see if they reach back. Stealthily, guiltily, we take in a sense of being protected and liked.

If we dare to feel or express a need and receive no

response, we become inarticulate, frozen in shame. If the other person notices the misstep in the relational dance and makes space for the need, the unexpected repair alters our deep expectation of abandonment and disintegration.

Entangled shame. Shame, contempt, and worthlessness sneak into our interactions despite our best efforts. Sometimes we can see that someone is projecting their shame on us, and we can do our best to hold that gently, and keep our distance when we need to. Sometimes we project our shame on others, and they can see it as well.

Sometimes we get entangled in a mutual shame projection, as if two Japanese puzzle boxes were locked together. Our shamed reactions trigger theirs in a loop, and the relationship becomes painfully difficult and confusing.

Even when we try to own our projections, we cannot own disintegration. As hard as we try, we cannot seem to fix the other person, or ourselves, or the situation. We struggle with trusting our perceptions about how best to protect ourselves. We want to flee the pain, and at the same time something inside says to pay attention, and wait.

Note: If you feel a clear impulse to leave, pay attention to that. It is not healing to override your perceptions of danger to stay in a situation because it might be "good for you."

Make room for change. The small shifts of healing shame can be preceded by a miserably long period of feeling stuck. Here are some suggestions to make room for change.

- Reach for outside support. Listen for feedback that honors your process and bolsters your self-trust.
- Generously assume good will when there is room for doubt.

- Invite each other to be on the same side.
- Offer small gifts of trust, vulnerability, and kindness.
- Step away when you need to.
- Watch for small changes in the stuck pattern, and welcome them.
- Stay grounded in your truth. You cannot heal shame by abandoning yourself.
- Forgive yourself for enacting shame, including abandoning yourself. You are doing your absolute best to relate and heal.

Shame says, we should be able to solve the puzzle of a mutual tangle more easily and quickly. Shame says, figure out who to blame and apply the rules about when to stay and when to leave. When nothing works, and we sit with the boxed-in frustration of that, eventually our deep implicit rules about relating begin to change.

Sparse network. Shame says we do not deserve to take up space, and we do not matter to anyone. Even when we feel isolated, we are more connected than we realize. Our brief kindnesses live in others' memories, as theirs live in ours. Our presence matters, even when it is unacknowledged. We can grieve for the dense network of support we want, and still acknowledge the sparse network we have.

Take some time to sense into the space you would leave behind if you decided to leave town. Who would you have to notify? Who would miss you when you did not come around after a while? What if you left your online "neighborhood" as well?

Too often we do not tell people how they matter to us until they are leaving, or we regret what is left unsaid when they are gone. Consider asking someone to tell you how you matter to them. Consider letting people know how they matter to you, perhaps with an email or hand-written thank you note.

You deserve to exist exactly the way you are right now. You deserve to have your physical and emotional needs met. You deserve soothing when you are in distress and celebration when you are joyful. How you were treated in the past was not your fault, and does not predict how you will be treated in the future. Invite yourself to breathe in as if you deserve to take up space in the world.

Resources

Your Body Knows the Answer: Using Your Felt Sense to Solve Problems, Effect Change & Liberate Creativity, Shambhala, 2014, by David I. Rome has practical step by step techniques for hearing ourselves and others with kindness.

Blindspot: Hidden Biases of Good People, Bantam, 2016, by Banaji and Greenwald offers clear, readable proof that good people exhibit hidden biases.

Why Are All the Black Kids Sitting Together in the Cafeteria: And Other Conversations About Race, Basic Books, 2003, by Beverly Daniel Tatum, Ph.D. is a careful, positive, hopeful introduction to thinking and talking constructively about race.

Martin Seligman writes about his classic experiments on learned helplessness in his book *Learned Optimism: How to Change Your Mind and Your Life*, Vintage, 2006.

In her book *Understanding and Treating Chronic Shame: A Relational/Neurobiological Approach*, Routledge, 2015, Patricia A. DeYoung explains her definition of shame and how to help people heal with compassion. She includes both lively client stories and dense psychological theory.

7: Relating

Relating with others can be an ongoing source of both trauma and healing. We need connection and attunement throughout our lives. Our attachment needs may smolder underground, suppressed by the mistaken belief that abuse is caused by trust and neediness, rather than by other people's bad behavior.

When our nervous system is in emergency mode, much of our capacity to relate is shut down. When the emergency is finally over, we can once again perceive and send the subtle signals of relating. At first we struggle primarily with relating to ourselves. Over time, our focus widens to relating with others, individually and in community.

Relationships of all kinds, from neighbors to coworkers to romantic partners, form a laboratory to practice boundaries, communication, and attunement. When we can accept ourselves as we are in the moment, we can advocate for our needs. When we can listen to our emotions, we can more easily navigate other people's defensive reactions as well as our own. When we can tolerate shame, we can apologize gracefully when needed, and allow other people to repair their missteps with us.

Attachment needs are part of our life-force. We can trust ourselves as we manage issues that arise with adult attachment relationships. We can listen to our anger as it signals boundary violations. We can stay aware of consent in a wide range of situations. We make the best decisions we can with the resources we have.

A Japanese tradition fills in the cracks of pottery with gold, both strengthening the damaged place and honoring the scar.* As we do the emotional labor of showing up with ourselves and others, we fill in trauma's cracks with the gold of presence.

---

* "Japanese Bowl," song by Peter Mayer, video by John Vandermey. youtube.com/watch?v=qOAzobTIGr8

Sensitivity Survival Tips

Sensitivities encourage us to express our boundaries and needs as we relate to others. We are all sensitive to physical and emotional toxins at some level. Some people start out nearly impervious, while others are sensitive to microscopic amounts.

When body and spirit are subjected to repeated or extreme trauma, we lose the ability to absorb further insults. The nervous system becomes reactive to smaller amounts of toxins, and interprets some non-toxic substances as threats. Most intolerances are not technically allergies, since they are not a histamine response, but the body is similarly trying to protect itself. Emotional and physical triggers vary from person to person.

New skills. Abusive environments teach us to keep our heads down and our mouths shut. The more we blend in with the background, the less we attract toxic attention. Yielding and adapting help us survive.

Sensitivities and intolerances challenge us to learn new skills. Faced with days or weeks of misery after each exposure, we begin to assert our body's needs rather than go along with the crowd. Gluten intolerance requires us to pre-screen restaurants and carefully quiz the server about ingredients. Chemical sensitivity requires us to request fragrance-free announcements in advance and leave events abruptly when fragrances are present.

New skills take both planning and practice. It is difficult

to think creatively in the grip of an adverse reaction. Symptoms often include anxiety, confusion, and fogged thinking, making it difficult to take steps to protect yourself.

In advance:

- **Establish a safe home base.** Minimize triggers as best you can. Think about one step you can take to make your home base a little safer for you.
- **Follow routines** for being away from home base. What can you bring with you to improve your experience? For example, I bring my own food to many events.
- **Contact new people and places ahead of time** to explain your needs. Tell allies how they can help.
- **List specific symptoms** during and after exposure. For example, with exposure to chemicals I get disoriented and can no longer tell right from left, have trouble remembering names, and get suddenly tired. Later I get joint pain and headaches.
- **Make an escape plan** in case your sensitivities get triggered.

During an event. You decided to attend an event and did what you could to minimize the risks. Now is your chance to relax and enjoy it. If you notice specific symptoms from your list:

- **Validate** for yourself that you are having a reaction.
- **Reach out to allies** if they are available.
- **Monitor** your symptoms. You might decide to

stay because you enjoy the event, or your attendance is required, or you lack the energy to set a boundary in that moment. Those are all valid reasons not to leave immediately.

- **Follow your escape plan** when symptoms outweigh your reasons to stay.

After a reaction:

- **Return** to your home base.
- **Give yourself time** to rest and recover.
- **Remind yourself** that your body is processing a toxic reaction and the symptoms will pass, although it may take several days or longer.
- **Practice self-care.** Take hot baths, drink extra water, or whatever you have noticed mitigates symptoms for you. Keep a list of actions you can take.
- **Look back with compassion.** Navigating boundaries and sensitivities is challenging.
- **Notice incremental improvements.** Did you see your symptoms with more kindness? Reach out to an ally sooner? Make a conscious decision to stay and pay the price later? Get yourself out of the situation even though it took longer than you wanted?
- **What made this situation difficult** and got in the way of self-care? Modify your symptom list and escape plan to take new information into account.

Find allies. Advocating for yourself takes extra energy you might not always have. Do you know other people with sensitivities who can share some of the work and validate your experience? Do you know sympathetic people who are not affected by the same triggers and can help you recognize symptoms and manage a reaction?

Handle non-allies. Sometimes people react in unhelpful ways to people with sensitivities. Instead of responding with compassion, they become defensive and focus on themselves. In particular, many fragranced products are marketed to cover body shame, leading people to feel attacked when asked to put them aside. We all have moments when defensiveness wins over compassion.

Some possible responses to unhelpful comments:

- **"I don't smell anything."** Acknowledge the comment as a simple statement about their senses. It has no bearing on the fact that you are having a reaction and need to leave. Do not allow them to gaslight you about what you sense in your environment and in your body.
- **"Smell me! Is it me?"** Redirect the person to an ally, or simply refuse. Taking deep breaths of possibly-scented air is the last thing you want to do.
- **"I'm grateful I don't have your problems."** This is rude. You can tell them that, firmly change the subject, or wait for them to wind down, depending on the situation and your energy level.
- **"It's all in your head."** This is even more rude, and might be phrased more subtly. A possible response is, "Respecting my limits works better for me than ignoring them."
- **"You need to get that fixed."** Your medical decisions are your private domain. Sensitivities are not well understood, and it can be hard to find

gentle treatment that helps rather than further irritating your nervous system.

- **Lack of respect for boundaries.** This might manifest as wearing fragrances, carelessness with gluten contamination, or otherwise exposing you to a trigger. In the moment, focus on self-care. In the future, avoid being vulnerable to that person or institution.

Grateful for boundaries. Recently a couple of people admired my boundaries when I left an event because of fragrances. I am grateful to my sensitivities for forcing me to prioritize self-care over appeasing others. Sometimes I also feel angry about the limitations imposed by our culture's toxic habits.

Take some time to notice all your complex emotions about being more sensitive than people around you. Are there any changes you want to make in how you handle that? Some triggers probably affect you less than others around you. Are there any changes you want to make in how you handle that?

Listen to Defensiveness

Like a heavy shield, defensiveness has its uses, and can also get in our way. Defensiveness can protect emotional wounds left by trauma and abuse. At the same time, it blocks out the rest of the world. In conversations, defensiveness prevents connection and communication.

While we quickly notice defensiveness in others, we are slower to notice and acknowledge it in ourselves. We become defensive when we feel threatened, or when we are trying to protect ourselves from shame or fear.

Explore your reactions. Imagine someone just accused you of stealing a cookie. Notice how your body feels in response. You might feel your shoulders hunch, your legs twitch, or your chest puff out. Denials, excuses, or counter-attacks might fly to your lips. You might feel angry, anxious, or defeated.

Is your internal feeling of defensiveness familiar? What happens when you acknowledge your response? "Something in me feels defensive and I say hello to that." Take some time to listen inside and get to know your defensive reactions. What sensations, images, or stories come to mind? Your defensiveness gets to be there as long as it needs to. Say hello to any judgments that come up as well.

Defense against change. Like denial, defensiveness helps slow down change. We cling to the familiar and defend the status quo, especially when it gives us power. When we acknowledge defensiveness, it gives us room to grieve for our losses. With time, we can open into curiosity and adapt to change.

Defense against shame. Defensiveness often arises when our self-image is threatened. We strenuously avoid the shame, embarrassment, humiliation, and self-hatred that arise when we fall short.

For example, when someone confronts us about a boundary transgression, it challenges our image as a good person. When we have more privilege and power than the challenger, we have access to a lot of tools to defend us. We might protest that we aren't like that, or there must have been a misunderstanding, or they did something wrong first. We might criticize their tone rather than addressing the content of their message. We might shut down conversation by changing the subject, leaving the room, or ignoring their communications.

Unfortunately, those tools cause further harm by erasing the challenging person's experience. They place more importance on our self-image than on someone's pain. The challenger may repeat the message with more intensity in an effort to get through, or may give up and go away mad, but there is no resolution.

Acknowledge defensiveness. When we feel our defensiveness flare up, we can pause to silently acknowledge our feelings. We might even name them out loud. "Wow, I'm feeling defensive." Acknowledgment brings relief and space to choose our actions. We can choose to listen to a challenger's experiences and pain. When we acknowledge the importance of their message, we begin the process of resolution.

Paradoxically, it is harder to behave like good people when we are busy defending our status as good people.

Defense against external threats. Sometimes we feel defensive because someone intentionally targets a vulnerable area. Defensiveness can alert us to subtle bullying or manipulation.

The first step is the same. We pause to acknowledge our inner experience, including feeling defensive. We silently affirm our right to be vulnerable, and to be treated with kindness. This creates space to identify why we feel threatened and choose our response.

If it is unclear why we feel defensive, we can choose to address the content of the communication. In some situations, we might also name our discomfort out loud. For repeat offenses, we can express a boundary, avoid the attacker, or look for allies.

For example, we might notice defensiveness in response to a prying question. We can protect our privacy by simply not answering. "Why do you ask?" or "It's complicated," or silence are all valid responses.

Other people's defensiveness. When we accept our defensiveness as a natural response to feeling threatened or ashamed, it becomes easier to handle defensive responses in others. It still hurts when they shut us out, but we know the response is about their internal reactions, not about us.

Focus on the goal. During a difficult conversation, we can focus on our goal, whether it is to convey a boundary, establish a better working relationship, or salvage a friendship. When we acknowledge defensive responses and then re-emphasize the goal, they may be able to set defensiveness aside and listen. Even if they remain defensive, we can avoid getting entangled in rejecting or soothing their defensiveness.

We can choose to speak our message once and stop, even

if the recipient gives no acknowledgment. Many people behave defensively in the moment, but then mull over new information later.

We can also choose to respond with the same message no matter what the person says. This can be useful for business transactions. For example, "I need to close my account," repeated calmly in the face of questions and objections.

Post-conversation self care. When we encounter defensiveness, not only is our message not acknowledged, but we may receive painful attacks as well. It can be triggering to be ignored, and dissociation can make it difficult to stay on track in the face of defensive distractions.

After a difficult conversation, we can come back to center with meditation, journaling, movement, or venting with a friend.

Rather than obsessing about how to get our message through next time, we can choose to believe, "This problem is already solved." The person might have heard us, and if not, we will find out soon enough.

If an angry attack still stings, we can reverse "I" and "you" in the painful statement. If someone says "You're so selfish!" notice whether they behave selfishly. Defensive speeches usually reveal more about the speaker than the recipient. We can also inquire inside whether some part of us believes the attack, and say hello to that part. Listen for sensations, images, or stories around that belief.

Commit to listening. When we commit to listening inside for our defensiveness, we can communicate more clearly with the people around us. If they remain defensive, we can respond with empathy for our shared humanity rather than entering into battle.

Apologies: Good, Bad, and Abusive

When we regret a defensive outburst, we can mend fences with an apology. Carefully crafted apologies can open the door to healing reconnection, or, with different intent, open the door to continued abuse. Their power comes from phrasing, nonverbal signals, and the surrounding context of the interaction.

We are all learning. Few of us learned about good apologies growing up. Instead of modeling genuine apology, many parents force children to voice a sullen, "I'm sorry," often followed by an unspoken, "… that I got caught." Did you receive apologies from adults as a child? What were they like?

In abusive environments, apologies are often associated with weakness and shame instead of connection and healing. As you read about apologies, do you notice shame or other emotions arising?

An apology acknowledges the speaker's boundary violation or transgression against someone, either spontaneously or in response to an expressed boundary. "I'm sorry that happened to you," or "I'm sorry to hear that," are expressions of sorrow and sympathy rather than apologies, and are not covered here.

Good apology: Focused on the recipient. A good apology focuses on the recipient's emotions and the speaker's actions. It expresses authentic regret, takes responsibility, and stops. The speaker then actively listens to anything the apology recipient wants to say.

"I'm sorry I'm late. I know it's annoying to be kept waiting. Next time I'll leave earlier." This creates room to talk about how it felt to wait. The recipient may feel relief, and a sense of being seen.

Good apologies validate the importance of the recipient's experience. For small transgressions, they nourish connection. For big transgressions such as past abuse, they can lift a burden of self-blame and confusion by making it clear the abuse was never the recipient's fault.

Bad apology: Focused on the speaker. Bad apologies focus on the speaker's feelings and make excuses rather than taking responsibility. "I'm so sorry I'm late! I feel terrible to keep you waiting, but traffic was snarled and I'm so busy these days." This is all about the speaker and leaves no room for the recipient's emotions. The recipient may feel annoyance, disconnection and a sense of being erased.

Another form of bad apology is "I'm sorry if you're offended," which evades responsibility for causing offense. Better options are, "I'm sorry I offended you," or "I'm sorry I phrased that offensively," or "I'm sorry. That was out of line."

Too many rain checks. Any repeated apology is a bad apology, no matter how carefully phrased. An apology is like a rain check promising future respectful treatment. If transgressions continue, repeated apologies are like a stack of rain checks for items that never come back in stock.

Abusive apology: Focused on control. Abusive apologies blame the recipient for what went wrong. Tone and body language convey a manipulative demand for appeasement or forgiveness. "I'm sorry I'm late, but you're the one who chose to meet at rush hour." The recipient may feel fear, anger, or distrust, and may reflexively apologize in turn to reduce tension.

An abusive apology can be stand-alone victim-blaming or part of a cycle of abuse.

Phase 1: Tension builds

Phase 2: Abuse occurs: emotional, physical, and/or sexual violence

Phase 3: Reconciliation, including abusive apologies

Phase 4: Calm, normalcy, until next time

Apologies mixed with boundaries. In the hall of mirrors of an abusive environment, a victim's attempt to both apologize and express a boundary can come out just like an abusive apology. "I'm sorry I snapped at you, but you kept interrupting me." Someone focused on control might respond, "That's not a proper apology!"

If you mix apologies with boundaries, take a step back and look at the power dynamics of the interaction. Consider separating your apologies from your boundary statements. "I'm sorry I snapped at you. I'm working on handling irritation differently." Then listen. In a separate conversation, you can say, "Interruptions make it hard for me to communicate."

"I'm sorry I exist." The shame of abusive behavior is often deflected onto the victims, who find themselves apologizing for anything and everything. Notice how often you apologize. Are you apologizing for existing, for taking up space, for having boundaries and preferences? Remind yourself that you never deserved abuse, and you have the right to take up space. Frequent apologies can be a holdover from past abuse, or a sign of lack of safety in the present.

In sexist environments, women are judged for apologizing

frequently, and at the same time strong women are judged for not apologizing enough.

Dream apologies. Many abuse survivors carry a dream that the perpetrator will finally see the survivor clearly, be horror-struck at causing pain, and issue a heartfelt apology. Those dreams rarely come true, but contain a seed of truth: each survivor's underlying faith in deserving care rather than abuse.

Are you waiting for someone to apologize to you? Write a letter to yourself with exactly the apology you desire. This is what you know you deserve. How does it feel to read it and take it in? Can you allow more of that feeling in your life, even though the transgressor remains unapologetic?

Is there an apology you carry inside about a past transgression you committed against someone else or yourself? Write it down, expressing your genuine regret and taking responsibility for what happened. How does it feel to put your regret into words? If it would do no harm to you or to the recipient, consider sending your apology, even if a lot of time has passed.

Forgiveness not required. When you receive an apology, no matter what kind, stay connected with how you feel. You may notice relief, annoyance, fear, or a mixture of emotions. You do not have to forgive in response to an apology. Forgiveness is private and internal, and happens in its own time. "Thank you" is a sufficient response, until and unless you want to share more about your truth.

As you give and receive apologies with thoughtful care, you can repair connections in your life that nourish you. Awareness of your internal responses helps you notice when apologies play a manipulative role.

Loving Anger

Carmen and Harrison have struggled through repeated fights and apologies.

Harrison says, "When you yell at me, you're abusive."

"Then obviously we need to break up." Carmen knows it would do no good to explain that she yells because he ignores her when she speaks calmly. Harrison has manipulated her into staying during past breakup attempts, but this time she is sure. Her rule is, if someone feels abused in a relationship, they need to leave.

Privately, she wonders, "Is raising my voice always abusive? What about self-defense? What's the right way to be angry?"

External and internal power. Anger is powerful. It can be used as an excuse for violence to gain power over others. Just the threat of anger can keep targets of abuse "in line."

Anger is also an expression of internal power and self-protection, a clear signal that our territory has been invaded. Anger can arise out of self-love and compassion for others when we react angrily to unfairness and injustice.

Value-neutral. Many of us feel ashamed of our anger and proud when we can avoid or suppress it. Our experience of anger can become layered with painful associations, braided with shame, fear, grief, or other intense emotions. Anger might trigger flashbacks to past trauma. When someone is angry with us, we might react with fear, preemptive surrender, or battle.

The emotion of anger is value-neutral, like any other emotion. It may feel unpleasant and inconvenient, but it is the truth of how we feel in the moment. It might also feel exhilarating and energizing. We can clamp down and hold it in place, or we can allow the energy to move through and make room for our next emotion.

Patterns of anger. We all experience anger in different ways. Some people flash into anger and out again like a summer storm, while some seem as immovable as a mountain until an avalanche rumbles into motion. Some people yell, some hit, some lift weights, and some stew in silence at 3 a.m. What do you notice about your patterns of anger?

Choices. The emotion of anger is separate from angry actions. Angry actions are not necessarily violent actions. When you feel anger, you can:

- **Respond** to any invasion that presents an immediate danger. Otherwise, take your time.
- **Pause to feel** this particular anger in your body. You may feel tightness in your jaw, cotton-wool in your throat, fire in your belly, or some other sensation. Does it change as you pay attention?
- Gently **listen inside** for the source of the anger. Whether it arises from the present, the past, or someone else's emotions, your experience of anger is valid. Within a Decision-Free Zone, compassionately listen for your full truth, including any violent impulses.
- Without abandoning yourself or making your anger wrong, can you **find empathy** for those you are angry with? Their behavior may be unacceptable, and at the same time, like you, they are doing the best they can with the resources

they have.

- **Explore your choices** for action, including doing nothing. What outcome would relieve your anger? What if that has already happened? What would someone who loves you do? What would someone you admire do? What do you wish you could do?
- **Consider leaning in**, holding your ground, or disengaging. Does the thought of one bring relief? You could ask someone to meet your expectations for respectful treatment, or lower your expectations of this specific person or situation to match what happened. When you have low expectations for a good outcome, how can you best care for yourself?
- **Consider both asking for help** and acting on your own behalf. Does the situation include a Drama Triangle, with a Victim, Perpetrator, and Rescuer? Can you witness it with kind curiosity?

Which options are familiar? Which are new? Predict what action will feel best when you look back on it, and notice how that turns out.

No perfect way. There is no one perfect way to handle anger. You do not have to be perfect. Women, people of color, and others lacking power in unbalanced relationships are often punished for showing anger. Painful double-bind messages convey that any anger is "too much" but calm speech can be ignored. Harrison's criticism of Carmen's yelling follows this pattern.

Fiercely defending your territory might be considered "unladylike" or "aggressive," but standing up for your boundaries is different from attacking someone else.

Unfortunately some people interpret boundary assertion as an attack and confusingly accuse you of attacking them, which is gaslighting.

Is anger abusive? When we notice violent impulses, we might worry about behaving abusively or turning into an abuser. While anger is often misused as a tool for abuse, it does not turn people into abusers.

Do you believe you are entitled to power and control over others? That is the underlying trait of abusive behavior. The more you view others with empathy, especially people you consider different from you, the less you are at risk for behaving abusively.

If you have acted in anger in ways you regret, consider whether an apology is in order. As you practice attending to your anger as a separate step from taking action, you will be less likely to act in ways you regret later.

"Here it is." Ideally, we would lovingly welcome anger like any other emotion. We can start by acknowledging its existence. "Here it is." Like Carmen, we may wonder how to best handle our anger. As we listen inside, explore options, and take self-protective action with empathy for others, we can build a solid relationship with our anger that works for us, as well as relate more easily to other people's anger.

Reasons to Stay

Many people think that the obvious answer to abusive relationships is to leave. We jump quickly to caustic victim-blaming of people who stay. "She must want it." "He must be trying to work something out in his past." "They lack the courage to make a change."

Patriarchal cultures are permeated by abuse. Every day, we fight abuse, flee abuse, and make compromises to meet our needs. Some people tolerate abusive work conditions for needed money. Some people tolerate abusive doctors for needed medicine. Some people tolerate abusive relationships for needed housing, respectability, or companionship. Some people buy products and services created in abusive conditions.

Life is complicated. People stay for the good parts, to learn something, to understand how they got there, to avoid going there again, or to fulfill an internal or societal story about what life and relationships look like.

Abusive situations are rarely clear-cut and unambiguous. An abusive spouse can also be genuinely loving at times, especially early in the relationship. The abuse may be subtle, laced with gaslighting so victims believe they are imagining or causing it.

If an abusive situation is unclear to the people involved, it is even less clear to outside witnesses. Even when a survivor does name abuse, mutual friends often refuse to "choose sides." This false neutrality compromises with an abuser to maintain comfortable community interactions for everyone except the survivor.

Safer to stay. Some people stay in abusive situations because they correctly assess that the abuser is more dangerous if they leave than if they stay. They stay to protect themselves and others they love from violence, blacklisting, and other reprisals.

Some people stay because they have (temporarily) surrendered their power to make choices and changes in their life. Learned helplessness is an injury caused by abuse. Any shame associated with it belongs to the abusers who caused it, not to the person who suffers through it.

Integrity. We make commitments to people and organizations without full knowledge of what is involved. Some abusers use the bait of intense love and care to encourage premature commitments, knowing that integrity will hold the victim in place for more abuse.

Society, the abuser, and the victim's Inner Critic say in chorus, "You haven't tried hard enough. You haven't fixed yourself yet. Have you looked at your part?" The victim continues to try harder instead of saying, "Wait, this isn't my fault at all."

Gradual change. Even when someone cautiously waits to make a commitment, a relationship can change over time. Gradually the balance shifts from occasional minor infractions ("no one is perfect") to larger blowups ("please forgive me") to ongoing abuse ("you provoked me"). It is painfully easy to believe that if we do the right thing, the relationship will change back to its pleasant beginnings.

Traumatic bonding. Abuse is rife with secrets and extreme experiences. This shared world forges a bond that is hard to leave behind, because it seems that no one on the outside will understand. Sadly, even the most extreme experiences are understood by many others in the world. Pain, trauma, and abuse are part of the human condition just as much as sunshine and rainbows.

In search of a door. We can fiercely and creatively seek non-abusive ways to meet our needs. Simply the act of looking can reveal a way out, or it can require years to pry open a door. Discrimination and injustice such as racism, sexism, homophobia, and economic inequality conspire to limit avenues for escape. Starting over is hard. Without access to money and social power, it can be impossible.

Disability and chronic illness can also limit available options, and can be intensified by abuse. Abuse causes depression, PTSD, vicious self-criticism, and bone-deep exhaustion. It is painfully easy to believe that if we are being abused, we deserve abuse, even though no one deserves abuse for any reason.

In process. Leaving is a process. From the outside, a decision to stay and a decision to leave look the same until the moment of separation. It takes many internal and external acts of preparation to build up to that moment.

Some people stay because they correctly assess that they do not (yet) have the emotional and physical resources to leave. Change and risk are frightening for everyone, especially when past risks have turned out badly. Waiting is a valid strategy in abusive situations.

Express your trust. If you know someone in an abusive situation, affirm that they are doing the best they can with the available information and resources. Express your trust in their essential strength and capacity to find their way. Help them notice what they are doing well.

Consider doing the same for yourself, if you are or have

been in abusive situations. How does it feel to send gentle encouragement back to a younger self?

Have compassion for your judgments and fears around people in abusive situations. It is difficult to witness someone's pain with the knowledge that they do not deserve it and there is no immediate solution.

Patience With Long Endings

Amirah and Galen are arguing again. This time, Amirah announces that she intends to go to prayer meeting at the mosque whether Galen approves or not, and Galen is welcome to come along if she wants. As usual, Galen has a reason to stay behind, and tries to convince Amirah to stay as well. To Galen's surprise, Amirah continues to get ready, and soon pedals off on her bike.

Amirah struggles with Galen's controlling behavior in their relationship. Some of her friends frown and tell her she should have left a long time ago. Part of Amirah agrees with them, and at the same time Amirah loves Galen and enjoys their time together. Every time she tries to decide firmly to go, or firmly to stay, she falls back into her internal struggle.

One boundary at a time. Recently, something shifted in Amirah. She told a couple of friends that, while she appreciates their concern, it hurts when they give her "shoulds" about her relationship. If they find it too hard to sit with her uncertainty, she won't discuss the relationship with them any more.

One friend angrily refuses to see her now. Amirah grieves the loss, and mutters to herself that boundaries should be allowed in friendships.

While her friends see relationships as either abusive or not, Amirah knows she is not in physical danger, and the emotional danger is subtle, complicated by past bad relationships with painful endings. She has time to sit with both wanting to go and wanting to stay. She wants to make room for a new solution that avoids painting Galen as an evil to flee or fight.

Room to adapt. Instead of trying to make a big final decision, Amirah looks inside for what she wants and needs, and finds the simplest steps to get there. She disengages from arguments, goes to the events she wants to attend, and continues to spend time with Galen.

As Amirah steps back from their usual dance, Galen has room to make her own decisions. She may adapt and learn to behave in a less controlling way. She may decide to leave now that Amirah is more assertive. Or Galen may remain unchanged, and Amirah might reach a point where she is done, or she might decide the relationship works well enough as it is.

Unpredictable future. From inside the relationship, Amirah has no way to predict how she will feel outside it. She might feel abandoned and ashamed for months, as she has after past breakups. She might feel light and relieved and happy. Her world might feel small, closed down by grief, or expansive, opened wide with new possibilities.

Clarity emerges. Over time, Amirah realizes that gaslighting is the biggest problem in the relationship. When she takes time to listen inside for her boundaries and preferences, she feels clear, calm, solid. After a conversation with Galen, she feels confused and self-critical, as if her perceptions do not make sense and her wants are wrong. Her preference becomes to spend less time with Galen, and she explains why.

When gaslighting continues despite several conversations about it, Amirah feels clear that she is done. During the breakup, they do their best to be kind to each other. Amirah experiences a mixture of grief and relief outside the relationship. Instead of feeling ashamed of a "failure", she feels proud that she made room to stay connected with Galen, and at the same time stayed centered in her own wants, needs, and perceptions.

Amirah finds that her boundaries have grown stronger through her practice of sitting with uncertainty, and taking steps to fulfill her wants and needs as they become clear. Like her disgruntled friend, not everyone is comfortable with the change. When the dust settles, she has fewer friends, a different job, and a continuing willingness to speak her truth.

Patience with uncertainty. As an outside observer, we might have strong opinions about what someone "should" do. They should obviously leave, because we see signs of abuse. They should obviously stay, because we see the benefits they receive. They should make a decision, because it is painful for us to see them uncertain and hurting. When we are the ones wondering whether to end a relationship, we internalize those judgmental voices.

From inside a relationship, as much as we want clarity now, we also have many reasons to stay. We might need to hear validation that certain behaviors are abusive, and that we deserve better. We might need to gather internal and external resources in preparation for leaving. We might need to patiently spend time listening to the parts in us that are done, and the parts in us that are not.

Negotiated endings. We tend to think of endings as being sudden, acrimonious, and final. While some are, we can often negotiate a more gradual change, or come to a mutual agreement that a situation is no longer a good fit. Some endings look sudden, but have built up over time, like a fraying strap that holds on until the final thread snaps.

We do not need to label a situation as abusive to leave. Sometimes, avoiding strong labels like "abusive" can make it easier to sense what we want and need, and make room for uncertainty.

Subtly abusive. Sometimes, the abusive label does fit, and it is validating to apply it to subtle situations. Abusive situations are rarely all bad, and rarely match our internal picture of "typical" abuse. Abuse happens in all sorts of relationships between all sorts of people. Our preconceptions about abuse get in the way of recognizing it when we feel or see it. Abuse causes a sense of shock at being treated as less than a whole, valued person. It can range from overt violence to subtle, corrosive disrespect.

After leaving, the situation often looks different from the outside. There might be immediate relief from ongoing difficulties that had become background noise. For example, getting away from negative feedback can be unexpectedly powerful. There might be recognition of benefits that had also faded into the background. We might breathe more freely once a decision is no longer hanging over us.

Skillful endings. Are you happy with how you navigate endings in your life? Most of us wish we could handle them more skillfully, with more compassion for ourselves and everyone else involved. We want permission to be angry, without resorting to violence. We want to walk away with confidence that those left behind will find their way.

We want to step lightly through minefields of old griefs and abandonments, while honoring present losses. We want to gracefully admit external defeat, and celebrate our internal successes around boundaries, self-care, and shifting out of old patterns.

We want gentle transitions, with a minimum of pain. We want to move smoothly away from identifying with what is ended, while making space to discover new or forgotten identities.

Rework an ending. While we cannot change the past, we can change how we carry our memories. Allow a past ending to come to mind, along with everything about it that makes you smile or wince. Say hello to its particular texture in your body.

How would you like this ending to be different? What would make it easier to carry? Take some time to invite in support you needed then, whether from your present self or some other assistance. What form does it take? Sense into how your body responds to the altered narrative. The changed texture in your body is yours to keep.

Interrupt existing patterns. CranioSacral Therapy helps the body find a new, healthier pattern of movement by gently preventing the current pattern. Held still and deprived of its habitual path, the body finds a new path with fewer restrictions. Sitting patiently with confusion or uncertainty serves a similar purpose. We interrupt our usual patterns, and wait for a new pattern to gradually emerge.

Enjoy Enthusiastic Consent

Consent is the key to respect in both personal and professional relationships.

Anyone who makes an appointment for bodywork, shows up, and lies down on the table has given consent to be touched, right? Wrong!

- Clients are in a vulnerable position relative to the practitioner, lying down, possibly with some of their clothes off. Even with active encouragement to express preferences, it can be hard to speak up.
- Some people bring themselves in for bodywork the way a parent drags a child to the doctor. They want their emotional and physical pain to stop, so they surrender their body to treatment while part of them is terrified.
- Some people wanted bodywork when they made the appointment, but encountered something triggering since then, and no longer want to be touched.
- Some people have never had their boundaries respected, and do not realize they have the right to choose what happens to their bodies in each moment. Returning that power to them is an important step in healing.

Start with a boundary check. For all those reasons, I start each session with a boundary check. Does this person on my table actually want to be touched? For some sessions, the boundary check is non-verbal and results in a clear affirmative. The client's body is relaxed into the table, and there is a sense of eagerness and welcome.

For some sessions, the boundary check is verbal: "I'm thinking of starting with your feet. How does that sound?" or "Do you have a sense of where you would like to start?"

Some sessions start with more formal work with boundaries, sensing the body's physical "no" and "yes" responses to proximity and touch, practicing saying no, and working with energy and words without touch. For many people, it is a healing challenge both to say no to unwanted touch, and to ask for what they do want.

Consent is an unforced moment-to-moment agreement to participate in a specific activity.

- **Unforced:** Any use of force nullifies consent. Force can be overt threats or violence, or covert manipulation, trickery, pressure, or intimidation.
- **Moment-to-moment:** Consent can be withdrawn at any time. Prior consent does not commit a person to continue consenting.
- **Agreement:** Consent is an active "yes", not just the absence of "no". Consent can be communicated non-verbally.
- **Specific:** Consent to one activity does not commit a person to consent to other activities.

Consent-based care. Some practitioners put the onus on their clients to say no to what they do not want, rather than checking in advance about what they do want. With an established routine, or an agenda to fix the client, interruptions and changes are resented as "resistance" rather than invited as part of healing.

Many clients have learned that compliance leads to receiving care, while expressing boundaries leads to subtle punishment and withdrawal of care. Consent-based care returns the onus to the practitioner to ensure that the client consents to each part of treatment. This is crucial for helping people heal from trauma, since trauma, which is unwanted and overwhelming, includes violation of consent.

Enthusiastic consent. Consent applies to all sorts of touch, including the non-sexual touch of bodywork. Enthusiastic consent applies more specifically to sexual activity. While there are edge cases where someone might less-than-enthusiastically consent to sex, we generally expect agreement to sexual contact to be clearly, enthusiastically affirmative for everyone involved.

Note: children cannot legally consent to sexual activity. Even if an adult gently sweet-talks a child into a sexual act, it is still assault. Children lack the understanding, physical maturity, and power to make unforced choices about sex.

Dissociation is not consent. For sexual activity, unconsciousness is not consent. Drunkenness is not consent. Dissociation is not consent. Sexual assault survivors may dissociate when sexual activity reminds them of an assault, or simply from the intense sensations of arousal. Holding to the standard of enthusiastic consent allows partners to notice when someone has dissociated, and stop.

Someone who is present and actively consenting will use words, sounds, and movements to indicate that. In stillness, they will be relaxed and responsive. Someone who is dissociated will be still, unresponsive, glazed, numb, or distracted. Movements are likely to be more stiff, jerky, or uncoordinated than usual. There is a sense of absence, and people around them might become distracted themselves.

Listen for a clear "yes." Some people argue that seeking enthusiastic consent interrupts and limits sexual activity. That argument supports rape culture, which normalizes sex with unclear consent. Enthusiastic consent counteracts the idea that some people (usually women) are supposed to avoid sex, and some people (usually men) are supposed to pressure others into sex. It gives everyone permission to discover and speak what they want and do not want.

Enthusiastic consent makes everyone responsible for listening for a clear "yes", rather than making a reluctant person responsible for expressing a clear "no". Too many rapes have been justified because the victim didn't say "no" clearly enough or loudly enough, according to the rapist.

In the bodywork realm of non-sexual touch, people might argue that seeking consent interrupts a massage. It is considered acceptable to continue massaging someone who falls asleep. At the same time, sleepiness can be a way to dissociate from discomfort. I periodically check in with clients even when they fall asleep.

Seek clear consent. We can hold to the standard of clear consent across our lives. For all our interactions, we can look inward for our preferences. As we state our boundaries and listen for other people's boundaries, it clears out relationships that depend on manipulation and hidden assumptions. It pits us against technology corporations that are greedy for our data. It gives us the clarity to leave when someone violates our consent, even in an unequal situation like a medical appointment. Over time, it sinks in that all of us deserve the respectful care of clear consent.

The Sacred Work of Showing Up

Emotional labor is the detail work of caring, of noticing, of paying attention. It is the foundation of strong relationships, and it is overwhelmingly gendered female. People perceived as women are expected to "naturally" do the work of keeping track and tending and nurturing, and are judged harshly for refusing. People perceived as men have the choice to remain oblivious that the work even exists to be done. More generally, people with less privilege are expected to care for people with more privilege.

Paid emotional labor includes the smile you get with your coffee from your regular barista, as well as their memory for what you always order. Many service workers are required to be warm, friendly, and enthusiastic as part of their jobs. Sociologist Arlie Russell Hochschild coined the term "emotional labor" in her 1983 book, *The Managed Heart: Commercialization of Human Feeling*.

Unpaid emotional labor in relationships includes the work of listening, keeping track of people's preferences, making sure everyone has what they need, remembering birthdays, sending thank you cards, and generally signaling, in a way that works for the recipient, that they are important and cared about. This work is a crucial part of creating community for everyone.

Comfort is a privilege. Unpaid emotional labor also includes tracking someone's emotional state from moment to moment, making sure they are not offended, soothing them if they seem upset, and looking for phrasing that is most likely to be acceptable to them. This work occurs when there is a power imbalance and a hidden threat of violence in a relationship. One person is doing the work of keeping another person on an emotional even keel.

It is an unequally distributed privilege to expect to be comfortable. It is a privilege to take for granted the work others do to create comfort, to expect others to discern and provide what pleases us without returning the favor. It is a privilege to expect people to prioritize moderating their tone to protect our tender feelings. Some messages are simply uncomfortable to hear.

Showing up. Doing our share of emotional labor includes showing up with ourselves, paying attention to our own behavior and emotions. It includes the gritty, exhausting, long haul work of healing from trauma. Looking inside is a service we do for ourselves, and also for the people around us. Each wound we heal, each old pattern we shift, each fractured child-self we integrate, helps us be more present, aware, and compassionate, which ripples out to benefit the rest of the world.

Doing our share of emotional labor includes showing up with others, identifying our longings, needs, and boundaries, and courageously talking about them. It includes listening to others' longings, needs, and boundaries and keeping them in mind in the future.

Pause and listen. When we talk about our emotional labor, we hope for recognition, appreciation, and, eventually, to share the burden. Unfortunately, people who are comfortably unaware of the emotional labor they demand often react with shame, anger, and defensiveness instead. The conversation turns once again to soothing their feelings, instead of being heard.

We can open the door to hearing uncomfortable truths by asking close friends or family, "Is there anything I take for granted that you would like to be appreciated for? Is there anything you want me to hear?" When someone says something surprising or jarring, we can resist reflexively telling them why they are wrong. Instead, we can pause and listen, showing respect for their viewpoint.

Look for balance. Emotional labor includes gentle attention to the balance between listening and talking. Our existing biases tend to reinforce imbalances. Those of us who have been taught to monitor the needs of everyone around us continue to believe we are not doing enough. Those of us who have been taught to expect our comfort to be prioritized continue to believe it is all someone else's problem.

Make the world a better place. Some people cause harm to others because they enjoy it, or think the ends justify the means. When most of us cause harm, we sincerely mean well, but we inflict our lack of awareness and unexamined patterns on the people around us.

When we show up with ourselves and others, when we peer into our shadows, when we learn to tolerate discomfort (but not misery), when we share responsibility for creating comfort, we add to the wholeness in the world. We begin to mend cultural and generational legacies of silence, aversion, neglect, and abuse, doing the sacred work of making the world a better place.

Resources

In *Taking the War Out of Our Words: The Art of Powerful Non-Defensive Communication,* Wyatt-MacKenzie Publishing, 2009, Sharon Ellison analyzes defensiveness and offers three strategies to communicate non-defensively: sincerely curious questions, vulnerable statements, and careful predictions. More information at PNDC.com.

In *I Thought We'd Never Speak Again: The Road from Estrangement to Reconciliation,* Harper Perennial, 2003, Laura Davis offers concrete suggestions for evaluating the possibility of reconciliation and moving toward it, including the role of apologies.

Helping Her Get Free: A Guide for Families and Friends of Abused Women, Seal Press, 2006, by Susan Brewster is a practical, compassionate guide when you know someone who is being abused.

Trauma Stewardship: An Everyday Guide to Caring for Self While Caring for Others, Berrett-Koehler Publishers, 2009, by Laura van Dernoot Lipsky with Connie Burk is about self-care around trauma work. The techniques of self-inquiry, presence, boundaries, and incremental change apply to endings as well as to working with trauma.

Olivia K. Lima's compilation document of the MetaFilter post "Where's My Cut?: On Unpaid Emotional Labor" contains 52 pages of validating, illuminating comments. drive.google.com/file/d/0B0UUYL6kaNeBTDBRbkJkeUtabEk

Hold Me Tight: Seven Conversations for a Lifetime of Love, Little, Brown & Co., 2008 by Dr. Sue Johnson explains adult attachment and gives concrete tools to save and enrich relationships.

Afterword: Presence After Trauma

After an emergency, the first task is to realize that it is over. As the nervous system and fractured parts become convinced, the longer, ongoing task is to build the life we want and fill in the gaps of skills and resources we missed.

I wrote "When I Started" (page 59) at a low point, when a lot of goals seemed out of reach despite all my efforts to be present in my body and my life. A wave of flashbacks and integrations, as well as continuing chronic pain and sensitivities, made it seem like the hard times would continue indefinitely.

A couple of years later, the flashbacks and chronic pain have eased, my body seems more resilient, my practice is as busy as I want it to be, and I am tentatively involved in a relationship. It reinforces my favorite saying for desperate moments (and years). "I give thanks for help unknown already on the way."*

When your process is not easy, when your life is not flowing as you would wish, when another wave of flashbacks strikes *again*, I hope you remember that it is not your fault,

---

* Author unknown, often credited as "Native American Prayer"

and you do not need fixing.

I hope that eventually, perhaps not in the shape you expect, you find the support you need and the kind of life you want and deserve. I hope you come to an understanding, a wary peace with all of who you are.

When we do the hard work of healing ourselves, we make the world a better place, not just for ourselves, but for everyone. Thank you, yes you, exactly who you are right now, for making the world a better place for all of us.

Does this book spark a response in you? I'd love to hear about it! Send your thoughts to sonia@TraumaHealed.com.

Glossary

Some glossary entries refer to my previous book, *Wellspring of Compassion*, abbreviated *Wellspring*. You can also find the referenced articles online at <u>TraumaHealed.com/articles/by-topic/</u>.

Ableism — Discrimination or prejudice against people with disabilities. Many common metaphors are ableist. For example, "blind" for unaware, "lame" for poorly executed, "crazy" for mean, bad, or unwise. See "Truth Across Lines of Authority" on page 189.

Acceptance — Saying hello to all aspects of our present experience, including the parts we hate and the parts we are ashamed of and the confused muddle we cannot even sort out into parts. See "2: Acceptance" on page 41.

ACE — Adverse Childhood Experience such as sexual assault, or incarceration of a parent. See "Not Alone with Your ACEs" on page 117 and "Appendix 1: Find Your ACE Score" on page 271

Activation — Tension and increased stress, "fight, flight or freeze" response of the sympathetic nervous system. See also **Settling**. See "Anxiety, Your Relaxation Coach" in

Wellspring, page 197.

Attachment — A loving bond between child and carer, or between two adults. See "Name Memories Without Words" on page 121.

Avenue of expression — Your jaw, tongue, throat, and the surrounding muscles and bones that support you in making sound to communicate your thoughts and emotions. Physical movement in your avenue of expression creates sound. Immobility is silent. See "Let Your Jaw Speak" on page 89.

Boundaries — A flexible container for sensations, emotions, and preferences, separating "me" from "not-me". See "Say Yes to Your Boundaries" in *Wellspring,* page 178.

Bullying — Repeated, aggressive acts in the context of a power imbalance. See "Interrupt Bullying" on page 197.

Chakra — One of seven energy centers along the front of the spine from tailbone to crown. See "Check In With Your Chakras" on page 29.

Cis — Short for cisgender (opposite of transgender), used to describe someone whose gender identity matches their anatomical gender at birth. See "Change the Rules, Inhabit Your Pelvis" on page 101.

Complex PTSD — A disruption of our fundamental sense of who we are, where we belong, and how we relate to others, caused by ongoing trauma. See "4: Trauma Effects" on page 115.

Consent — An unforced moment-to-moment agreement to participate in a specific activity. See "Enjoy Enthusiastic Consent" on page 253.

Decision-Free Zone — A safe time and space to listen to all of yourself, with a clear boundary that action is off the table. See "Decision-Free Zone" on page 19.

Developmental trauma — Ongoing violation and/or abandonment by trusted people during childhood. See "4: Trauma Effects" on page 115.

Dissociation — Spaciness, disconnection, feeling distant from current experience. See "Gain Awareness of Dissociation" in *Wellspring*, page 164.

Double bind — A situation where any choice leads to punishment, you can't leave, and you can't discuss the situation. See "Step Away from Double Binds" in *Wellspring*, page 128.

Drama Triangle — Three interlocked roles of Victim, Rescuer, and Persecutor. People involved in the drama can fluidly shift roles, or all three roles can be internal to one person. See "Compassion for the Drama Triangle" in *Wellspring*, page 196.

Emergency mode — A state of urgency and panic that continues after a traumatic event even though safety has been restored. See "Exit Emergency Mode" on page 134.

Emotional abuse — Words, body language, and other behaviors that bully someone into feeling defective. See "Emotional Abuse: You Deserve Better" in *Wellspring*, page 129.

Emotional labor — The detail work of caring, of noticing, of paying attention. See "The Sacred Work of Showing Up" on page 257.

Everyday gaslighting — Not acknowledging someone's words, actions, or perceptions, which is crazy-making. See also **Gaslighting**. See "Trust Yourself Despite Everyday Gaslighting" on page 177.

Faith — Your deepest certainties and longings about your connection with Spirit. See "Spiritual Abuse: Take Back Your Faith" in *Wellspring*, page 131.

Flashback — Intrusive sensations, emotions, and reactions from the past which impinge on a trauma survivor's present-day life. Flashbacks are a hallmark symptom of **PTSD**. See also **Trigger**. See "Flashbacks: Experience Distress in Safety" in *Wellspring*, page 211.

Flashback hangover — A feeling of rawness and fragility for a few hours or days after experiencing a **flashback**.

Flashback markers — Words such as "never," "always," or "forever" that indicate an experience, thought, or emotion is frozen in time. See also **Flashback**.

Focusing — A simple method for connecting with yourself. When you notice a sensation or emotion, you can keep it company, listening for its truth without expecting it to change. See "Repair Your Reality After Gaslighting" on page 172.

Freeze — Physical collapse, stillness, and dissociation from the body in response to an overwhelming threat with no possibility of overcoming it. See also **Surrender**. See "Frozen! Thaw from Surrender" in *Wellspring*, page 170.

Gaslighting — Psychological abuse that attempts to destroy the victim's trust in their perceptions of reality. See "Repair Your Reality After Gaslighting" on page 172.

Inner Critic — Internal voice that tells you everything you have done, are doing, and will do wrong. See "Calm Your Inner Critic" in *Wellspring*, page 46.

Inner Nurturer — Internal voice that knows you deserve care and respect and there is nothing wrong with you. See

"100 Percent On Your Own Side" in *Wellspring,* page 18.

Integration — The process of welcoming fractured parts of ourselves back into the whole. See "Integration: Live into Both/And" on page 71.

Kabbalah — An ancient Jewish tradition, including a Tree of Life that maps energy centers on the body. See "Weave Your Body Whole" on page 34.

Mansplaining — A man condescendingly explains to a woman something she already knows, and keeps talking even if she tries to correct his assumption. See "Trust Yourself Despite Everyday Gaslighting" on page 177.

Meditation — Sit comfortably, take three slow breaths, and notice what happens. Okay, now do it again. And again. There, you're meditating! See "Meditation: Safe Space for Noticing" in *Wellspring,* page 86.

Post-Traumatic Stress Disorder (PTSD) — A label for the nervous system's long-term response to trauma. Diagnostic symptoms include intrusive memories (**flashbacks**), avoidance and emotional numbing, and anxiety and increased emotional arousal. See "4: Trauma Effects" on page 115.

Presence — Sensing one's experience right now. See "Introduction: Welcome Back" on page 1.

Privilege — Unearned rights, advantages, and immunities given to people who fit into a specific social group. Privilege is the other side of oppression. See "Truth Across Lines of Authority" on page 189.

Projection — Assigning unwanted qualities to the people around us instead of acknowledging them within ourselves. See "Unhook from Projection" on page 46.

Red flag — A small boundary violation which could be a

warning sign for larger violations in the future. See "'Trust Me!' and Other Red Flags" in *Wellspring,* page 134.

Resilience — Ability to recover from shock or injury. Yielding and springing back into shape like a living tree branch. See "Heritage of Resilience" on page 157.

Resource — A source of support and strength. Resources can be external, such as a friend or a safe place, or internal, such as taking a deep breath to connect with the present moment. See "Remember at Your Own Pace" in *Wellspring,* page 167.

Ritual abuse — Prolonged, extreme, sadistic abuse in a group setting. Any ideology can be used to control group members, break their spirits, and justify torture. See "Spiritual Abuse: Take Back Your Faith" in *Wellspring,* page 131.

Sefira (plural Sefirot) — One of the ten energy centers in the Kabbalistic Tree of Life. See "Weave Your Body Whole" on page 34.

Self-care — Meeting yourself where you are right now with kind attention. See "Introduction: Welcome" in *Wellspring,* page 1.

Sensitivity — Awareness of and vulnerability to one's physical and emotional environment. See "Sensitivity Survival Tips" on page 227.

Settling — Relaxation and decreased stress, "rest and digest" response of the parasympathetic nervous system. See also **Activation**. See "Anxiety, Your Relaxation Coach" in *Wellspring,* page 197.

Shadow — We start out freely expressing all of ourselves, but quickly learn that some qualities are rewarded more than others. The qualities we push away, both positive and negative, accumulate into our shadow. See "Unhook from Projection" on page 46.

Somatic Experiencing® — Trauma healing techniques developed by Peter Levine. See "Heal Around the Edges" on page 10.

Spiritual abuse — When any abuser damages the victim's sense of worth, purpose, or connection to Spirit, or when a spiritual official causes harm to a congregation member. See "Spiritual Abuse: Take Back Your Faith" in *Wellspring*, page 131.

Surrender — Submitting to a threat. Waiting for an opportunity to resist. Letting go of internal resistance. See "Surrender Without Shame" on page 215.

Tone argument — Silencing someone with less power or privilege by criticizing their tone instead of listening to their message. The tone is often "too angry." See "Deflect the Tone Argument" on page 193.

Trauma — An event or ongoing situation which overwhelms a person's available coping skills. See "Signs of Trauma" in *Wellspring*, page 3.

Trigger — An internal or external experience that stimulates a traumatic memory. Triggers can come through any of the senses, or through a thought or emotion. They can be subtle, such as the light at a certain time of year. See "Triggered! Now What?" on page 138.

Victim-blaming — The belief that if victims had behaved differently, they would not be coping with bad news now, so it must be their fault. No one deserves abuse for any reason. See "Demand Respect, Not Victim-Blaming" in *Wellspring*, page 117.

Appendix 1: Find Your ACE Score

This Adverse Childhood Experience (ACE) Questionnaire allows you to find your ACE score. Note that while these 10 questions cover a lot of ground, they do not cover all types of childhood abuse, neglect, and catastrophe. Feel free to add points to your score for chronic toxic stress you experienced not covered in the questionnaire.

Note that trauma affects each person differently based on the internal and external resources and support available to them. See "Not Alone with Your ACEs" on page 117 for more information.

While you were growing up, during your first 18 years of life:

1. Did a parent or other adult in the household **often or very often**

Swear at you, insult you, put you down, or humiliate you?

or

Act in a way that made you afraid that you might be physically hurt?

Yes   No

2. Did a parent or other adult in the household **often or very often**

Push, grab, slap, or throw something at you?

or

Ever hit you so hard that you had marks or were injured?

Yes   No

3. Did an adult or person at least 5 years older than you **ever**

Touch or fondle you or have you touch their body in a sexual way?

or

Attempt or actually have oral, anal, or vaginal intercourse with you?

Yes   No

4. Did you **often or very often** feel that ...

No one in your family loved you or thought you were important or special?

or

Your family didn't look out for each other, feel close to each other, or support each other?

Yes   No

5. Did you **often or very often** feel that ...

You didn't have enough to eat, had to wear dirty clothes, and had no one to protect you?

or

Your parents were too drunk or high to take care of you or take you to the doctor if you needed it?

Yes   No

6. Were your parents **ever** separated or divorced?

Yes   No

7. Was anyone in your household:

Often or very often pushed, grabbed, slapped, or had something thrown at them?

or

Sometimes, often, or very often kicked, bitten, hit with a fist, or hit with something hard?

or

Ever repeatedly hit at least a few minutes or threatened with a gun or knife?

Yes No

8. Did you live with anyone whose overuse of alcohol and/or other drugs made them emotionally unavailable or dangerous to you?

Yes No

9. Was a household member depressed or mentally ill, or did a household member attempt suicide?

Yes No

10. Did a household member go to prison?

Yes No

Now add up your "Yes" answers. This is your ACE Score.

About the Author

Sonia Connolly offers intuitive, compassionate bodywork in Portland, Oregon for sensitive people healing from trauma. She is a survivor of incest, emotional abuse, and ritual abuse, and has sensitivities to gluten and fragrances. She finds joy in helping people heal, meditation, creativity, bicycling for transportation, gardening, petting her cat, and Balkan dancing and singing.

Learn more and sign up for free monthly healing articles at TraumaHealed.com.

Does this book spark a response in you? I'd love to hear about it! Send your thoughts to sonia@TraumaHealed.com.

Presence After Trauma

Illustration Credits

Cover photo, Crystal Springs Rhododendron Garden, Portland Oregon, by Sonia Connolly.

Chapter heading illustrations and sun by Laurel Purdy.

Kabbalah Tree of Life, page 34, modified from cliparts.co/clipart/3196399.

Psoas muscles, page 86, modified from diagram by BodyParts3D, © The Database Center for Life Science licensed under CC Attribution-Share Alike 2.1 Japan via en.wikipedia.org/wiki/Psoas_major_muscle.

Jaw muscles, page 91, modified from masseter and temporalis animated gifs generated by BodyParts3D, Copyright(c) 2008 Database Center for Life Science licensed by CC display – Share Alike 2.1 Japan via en.wikipedia.org/wiki/Temporal_muscle.

Thoracic spine, page 93, modified from diagram by BodyParts3D, Copyright(c) 2008 Database Center for Life Science licensed by CC display – Share Alike 2.1 Japan via en.wikipedia.org/wiki/Thoracic_vertebrae.

Bones of the shoulders, arms, and hands, page 98, modified from public domain diagram by LadyofHats via en.wikipedia.org/wiki/Arm.

Pelvis diagrams, page 102, modified from public domain plates from Henry Gray (1918) *Anatomy of the Human Body* via en.wikipedia.org/wiki/Pelvis.

Bones of the leg, ankle, and foot, page 106, modified from public domain diagram by A. Kopf via en.wikipedia.org/wiki/Human_body.

Chartres labyrinth, page 214, modified from original drawing by Robert Ferre, final graphic by Vicki Keiser via www.labyrinthsociety.org/download-a-labyrinth.

Lightning Source UK Ltd.
Milton Keynes UK
UKHW010818300721
387978UK00002B/523